Bible Plants and Animals

Bible Plants and Animals

Volume 3

PLANTS

Harry J. Baerg

REVIEW AND HERALD® PUBLISHING ASSOCIATION
WASHINGTON, DC 20039-0555
HAGERSTOWN, MD 21740

This book was
Edited by Gerald Wheeler
Designed by Bill Kirstein
Cover illustration by Harry Baerg
Cover calligraphy by Aaron Presler
Type set: 10 pt. Clearface Regular

Bible Texts credited to NIV are from the *Holy Bible, New Inter-
national Version.* Copyright©1973, 1978, International Bible Society. Used by permission of Zondervan Bible Publishers.

Bible texts credited to RSV are from the Revised Standard Version of the Bible, copyrighted 1946,
1952©1971, 1973.

PRINTED IN U.S.A.

R&H Cataloging Service

Baerg, Harry J.
    Bible plants and animals.
    3 v.

    Vol. 1, Mammals. Vol. 2, Birds
and other animals. Vol. 3, Plants.

    1. Bible—Natural History.   I. Title.
II. Title: Mammals. III. Title: Birds
and other animals. IV. Title: Plants.

        220.85

Library of Congress Cataloging in Publication Data

Baerg, Harry J.
    Bible plants and animals: natural history of the Bible / Harry J. Baerg.
        p.   cm.
    Contents: v. 1. Mammals
    1. Animals in the Bible—Dictionaries. 2. Plants in the Bible—Dictionaries.
3. Bible—Dictionaries. I. Title.
BS663.B34   1989
220.8'574—dc20   89-32937
                                                            CIP

ISBN 0-8280-0500-1

Flowers

FLOWERS OF THE FIELD (tzitz ha sadeh, pera, nitzah, nitzinim).
The Bible mentions only two flowers by name: the rose and the lily. However, the actual identity of both is uncertain. Scripture uses several general terms for flowers: "The flowers [nitzinim] appear on the earth" (Song of Solomon 2:12). David says in Psalm 103:15, "As a flower of the field [tzitz ha sadeh], so he flourisheth." And in Isaiah 40:6 we read, "All flesh is grass, and all goodliness thereof is as a flower of the field." Peter, too, dwells on the brevity of man's life, comparing it to flowers that bloom beautifully for a time, then vanish (1 Peter 1:24).

When Christ in the Sermon on the Mount spoke of the "lilies of the field," He, too, scholars tell us, had in mind flowers in general, rather than specifically the white lily that actually grows in the mountains of Palestine instead of the fields. Travelers who visit Israel in the spring remark about the number and beauty of the flowers that blanket the hills and fields for a few short months before they drop their petals and turn brown in the summer heat. We will here discuss briefly some of the flowers that the Bible writers may have included in the general terms used, but do not specifically mention. It is interesting to note that more red ones appear among them than any other color.

ANEMONE, CROWN; *Anemone coronaria*. 12"

Tradition holds that when Christ spoke of the "lilies of the field" in the Sermon on the Mount (Matthew 6:28 and Luke 12:27), He had the anemone in mind. It covers the hillsides and fields of many of the Mediterranean countries, especially Palestine, in a riot of red, white, purple, blue, and pink from early spring to the end of April. No doubt it was in profuse bloom then on the very hillside on which Jesus spoke.

Anemones belong to the buttercup family and are closely related to the wind flowers, or wood anemones, of the eastern United States, and also the lavender pasqueflowers that blanket the American prairies in early spring. They rise from a hardy coram, or bulb, that supplies them with stored food for the early blooms. The flowers usually have six petals, but may have more. While they have no nectar, many insects visit them for the abundant pollen borne by the numerous stamens. In this way they become cross-pollinated. The wind later disperses the winged seeds. Anemones grow almost everywhere in Palestine from the Negev Desert in the south to the cooler slopes of Mount Hermon in the north. The red crown anemone blooms from late winter to early spring and whole fields blaze with its color.

CHAMOMILE, DOG; *Anthemis nobilis. 8"*

The attractive dog chamomile could well have been a "flower of the field" found in Isaiah 40:6 or "flower of grass" mentioned in 1 Peter 1:24. In both instances the Bible writer compares man's life to the comparatively ephemeral nature of flowers that bloom today and wither tomorrow.

The chamomile is a daisy-like member of the large Compositae family, with bright yellow flower heads surrounded by white bracts. The blooms, though not large, are numerous and arise from a dense mass of finely divided, aromatic foliage. The flowers open in the morning and close their bracts in the evening.

People have long used both the flowers and the foliage for medicinal purposes. We grew them in our herb garden at home, and Mother made a tea for us from the flower heads when we were sick. They probably served the same purpose in Bible times. One can extract an aromatic oil from the plants. The flowers and leaves smell sweet but taste bitter. They can be made into poultices as well as tea and are said to be an antidote for spasms and toothache. The tea does increase perspiration, which can be beneficial.

CORNFLOWER, SYRIAN; *Centaurea cyanoides.* 12"

The common bachelor's button of our roadsides and gardens often grows as a weed in cornfields, and for that reason gets the name of cornflower. Its petals are blue, and the flower centers are more of a red-violet, but they also come in several other combinations of colors. The blossoms are usually about an inch across. In the Holy Land they bloom from February to May.

CROWFOOT, SCARLET; *Ranunculus asiaticus*. 8"

Another beautiful flower in the buttercup family in Israel is the scarlet crowfoot, also known as the turban buttercup. It blooms a little later than the anemone, but survives in some of the more arid parts of the country. Unlike the anemones, the crowfoot does not have an underground coram in which to store food, but has enlarged roots that serve the same purpose. In a country with only two seasons, the rainy and the dry, it is important for plants to store food during times of rain to draw on during the season of drought. Flowers must take full advantage of a short growing season. Beside the enlarged roots grow fibrous ones to absorb moisture quickly.

The crowfoot in many ways resembles our buttercups and crowfoots, but practically all of ours are yellow, while it is red. It gets its name from its narrow three-lobed leaves that resemble the foot of a crow.

DAFFODIL, SEA; *Pancratium maritimum.*

Along the shores of the coastal plain of Palestine the large, white blossoms of the sea daffodil, or sea pancratium, shoot up from the sand even before the beginning of the rainy season. Because they are so striking and appear before most other flowers, some scholars believe they are the "rose of Sharon." Still others identify them with the "lilies of the field."

The sea daffodil is a flower of the amaryllis family, quite a number of which we keep in our flower gardens and as indoor plants. Several large, white flowers appear at the top of a stout stem that shoots up about a month before the bladelike leaves appear.

DAISY, CROWN; *Chrysanthemum coronarium. 30"*

Here is another plentiful "flower of the field" whose bright-yellow blooms grow in dense masses and often take over whole fields and roadsides. The blooms resemble our garden and florist varieties of mums. Most of the domestic varieties of chrysanthemum have originated from two wild species in the Asia Minor region.

Crown daisies are annuals, reseeding themselves year after year. In Palestine the brilliant flowers appear in March and April rather than during the fall as they do here.

IRIS, NAZARETH; *Iris palestina.* 10″

This low-growing, spreading iris begins to bloom around Nazareth as early as the month of February. Its style of growth enables it to withstand the cold winds that blow at that early season. The irises come in several different colors, and each variety has its own environmental niche where conditions are just right for its needs. The Nazareth iris is neither a desert nor a Mediterranean plant, but seems to prefer regions just between the two. Some of the Palestinian irises grow quite a bit taller than the Nazareth species, more like the ones we have in our gardens.

LILY, WHITE (shoshan, shushan, havatzeleth) (krinon); *Lilium candidum.* 45"

Suggestions as to what Christ had in mind when He used the word *lily* in His sermon on the mount have ranged from the lotus, tulip, anemone, fall crocus, Turk's cap lily, buttercup, and iris, to the gladiolus. But lilies do live in Palestine, hugging the slopes of Mount Carmel, and in Galilee. Although rare now, they may have been more plentiful in Bible times. They are not, however, "lilies of the field," for they grow in the mountains. The Hebrew word *havatzeleth*, even though Isaiah 35:1 of the Revised Standard Version translates it as crocus, should, according to some, have been rendered "lily."

The lily provided a design to adorn the capitals of the freestanding pillars in front of Solomon's Temple (1 Kings 7:15-20). To the Jews it symbolized beauty and fertility, but in the Christian church it has come to represent holiness, purity, and hope. From that it has become associated with the Resurrection and the celebration of Easter.

The white lily of Palestine is much the same flower as the Easter lily we see in florist's shops. At the top of its leafy stem is a cluster of pure white, tubular flowers with recurved petals, yellow stamens, and an orange-tipped style. They give off a strong perfume, especially at night. The scent attracts the sphynx moths to the white blossoms, where they cross-pollinate the flowers as they search for nectar.

The most familiar text about lilies is "Consider the lilies . . . , how they grow; they toil not, neither do they spin: And yet I say unto you, That even Solomon in all his glory was not arrayed like one of these" (Matthew 6:28, 29). The lily also appears in Song of Solomon 2:1, 2: "I am the rose of Sharon, and the lily of the valleys. As a lily among thorns, so is my love among the daughters."

MALLOW—see Garden Plants

NARCISSUS—see Rose

POPPY, COMMON; *Papaver rhoeas.* 18"

The common poppy is abundant on the Palestinian hillsides in late spring. Probably David, Isaiah, Christ, and James had it in mind when they spoke of the fleetingness of human life. Its scarlet blooms last only a day or two, then the petals fall and the seed pods mature and ripen. The pores under the cap open up, and one can shake the seeds out and eat them straight or sprinkled on food as a seasoning. The sap of the unripe poppy head provides the source of opium.

The Palestinian poppies with their hairy stems and buds, resemble the ones listed in our seed catalog as Iceland poppies, but the flowers of the Palestinian species are all red with dark centers, whereas ours come in a variety of colors. They are annuals, growing each spring from the seeds dispersed by the nodding heads the previous summer. This accounts for the fact that they bloom later than most of the bulb flowers.

REICHARDIA—see Bitter (Herbs and Spices)

ROSE, PHOENICIAN (vered, chabasseleth); *Rosa phoenicia.* 36"

The word *rose* appears twice in the King James Version of the Bible. The Song of Solomon has the well-known text "I am the rose of Sharon, and the lily of the valleys" (2:1), and in Isaiah 35:1 is an equally familiar one, "The desert shall rejoice, and blossom as the rose." It is doubtful whether the translation of *chabasseleth* as "rose" is valid, and some more recent versions read "crocus" instead. Others have suggested the narcissus, the asphodel, and the primrose.

Narcissus tazetta covers the Plain of Sharon in November when the rainy season begins, and it could have been the "rose of Sharon" the Bible writer had in mind. This narcissus is a white flower with a lemon-yellow crown, similar to many of the other narcissi and daffodils. Palestine also has a number of different crocuses, but they are rather small and less showy. They bloom in the fall at the beginning of the rainy season and few consider them as a contender for the title of "rose of Sharon." The primrose is more a flower of cool damp climates and does not flourish as well in Bible lands. The asphodel, or daffodil, grows along the seacoast.

Real roses, however, do grow in Palestine. Four species, mostly alpine, inhabit mounts Hermon and Sinai, but one, the Phoenician rose, frequents the banks of rivers and streams. It has single, pink blossoms and looks much like the wild roses that border American roadsides. It is not likely, though, that it is what the Bible writer meant by the "rose of Sharon."

According to the Talmud, rose gardens of domesticated flowers have existed in Jerusalem from early times. People raised them to make perfumes and rosewater.

TULIP, MOUNTAIN; *Tulipa montana.* 18″
TULIP, SUN'S EYE; *Tulipa oculus solis.* 14″

Among the several species of tulips found in the Holy Land the mountain tulip and the sun's eye are the most prominent. Both are a showy red. The sun's eye thrives in the hill country, and its narrow leaves are some of the first to shoot out of the ground as the winter rains begin. The leaves of the mountain tulip have wavy edges. Gardeners have developed many of the present-day varieties of tulips in Holland from these Mediterranean species.

The "flowers of the field" we have mentioned did not all bloom at once, but in sequences that overlapped each other, beginning with some of the fall species through the winter to the earliest spring varieties down to the last of the poppies in May. During the summer the only flowers one finds are a few that grow on hardy trees. The rest of them have dried up as grass ready to be "cast into the oven" (Matthew 6:30).

Garden Plants and Field Crops

Scripture refers to a number of cultivated plants by name, some others by group names, and the existence of still others we can only infer by indirect ways. The Bible mentions only a few vegetables, among them leeks, onions, and garlic. Many vegetables so important to us now were unknown to the people of Bible times. They could not grow many of the cool climate plants such as the members of the cabbage family. Carrots, turnips, beets, and potatoes had not yet reached the Holy Land. Potatoes originated in South America, while most of the other common food plants come from northern Europe.

The Israelites did, however, have gourds and the related muskmelons and watermelons. Cucumbers, though mentioned by name in the King James Version, did not then grow in Bible lands. The broad beans, chick peas, lentils, and peas represented the pulses or legumes. The grains of the Israelites included wheat, barley, millet, and sorghum, most of which developed from native grasses. Corn, though mentioned by name in the KJV, actually refers to grain by its Old English name. What we refer to as corn today is strictly of American origin and thus unknown in Palestine during Bible times. A more precise term is maize.

Herbs and spices we have chosen to list in a separate category, since Scripture speaks about quite a number of them. They were apparently quite important to the people of that time.

BARLEY (seorah, seorim) (krithe); *Hordeum vulgare. 24"*

The terms for barley appear more than 30 times in the Scriptures, and without doubt it was one of the important cereals of the Biblical world. The barley harvest came about the time of the Passover and was one of the festive times of the year. The "wave sheaf" that figured prominently in the Feast of Unleavened Bread, the Passover, was a sheaf of barley, for that was the only grain yet ripe. We read that the plague of hail leveled the fields of barley and flax of the Egyptians, but left those of the Israelites untouched (Exodus 9:23-33).

Ruth and her mother-in-law came back to Israel from the land of Moab during the barley harvest, and she gleaned in the fields of Boaz (Ruth 1:22). The Philistines hanged Saul's sons after his defeat at the time of the barley harvest (2 Samuel 21:9).

Barley could serve, according to the Levitical laws, as a sacrifice. A homer of barley was valued at 50 shekels of silver when promised as an offering to the Lord (Leviticus 27:16). A man suspicious of his wife could subject her to a ritual involving the tenth part of an ephah of barley to determine whether she had been faithful to him or not (Numbers 5:14-28). Ezekiel also mentions "the sixth part of an ephah of an homer of barley" as an appropriate offering in the renewed land of Israel (Ezekiel 45:13). Hosea bought for himself as a wife an adulteress for 15 pieces of silver and 1 1/2 homers of barley (Hosea 3:2). The Bible mentions barley a number of times as food and as a gift for someone. Also we have the well-known story of the boy with the five barley loaves and two small fishes that Christ used in His feeding of the 5,000.

When I grew up on a prairie farm and we cultivated barley among our field crops, it was easy to tell the flat-headed, two-row barley from the wheat, because the barley had long, raspy awns (slender bristles that terminated the spike or beard of the barley) that broke off and got down our necks in harvesttime. The wheat we planted did not have awns. Now some varieties of wheat grown have awns and some of the barley, the six-row kind, does not. However, barley, as a rule, does not shell out of the hulls when rubbed in the palm as the wheat does.

Barley matures about a month earlier than wheat, and for that reason it is grown in drier areas than wheat. It will sprout during the early rains, and then mature and ripen about the time that the drought of summer begins. Palestinian farmers terraced the hillsides, even in early periods, to hold as much water from the winter rains as possible, and in that way they could grow barley even on some marginal desert land.

On our prairie farm we usually sowed barley on fields where wild oats were a problem. Ordinarily wild oats ripened before wheat, and much of it seeded out in the field before we could harvest the wheat, insuring a heavy infestation of the weed grain in the coming year. Barley sown in the field ripened even before the wild oats, and, when harvested the two got cut together, taken off the field, and threshed together. This prevented the oats from seeding out. We used the barley just for chicken and livestock feed anyway, and in this way we removed the wild oats from the field.

Today most of the barley grown in America goes for stock feed. We found that it is more fattening than either wheat or oats, but fed in the right proportions, it makes good feed. Much of the better barley grown gets used in the manufacture of malt, needed for making liquors and malted milk. Some becomes pot barley. The kernels are chafed in a revolving drum until it rubs away most of the hull. Pot barley becomes an ingredient of soups. It may be processed still longer to remove all of the hull and the germ, leaving little balls of starch known as pearl barley.

The people of ancient Palestine considered barley bread the bread of the poor, not only because one could grow it on poor soil with little rain, but also because it was difficult for farmers with their primitive methods to remove all the husks from the kernels, and the flour tended to be gritty. In addition, since it contains less gluten than wheat flour, the bread is heavier.

In feeding the 5,000 (John 6:9) Christ used the barley loaves brought by the boy for his lunch. They were not loaves as we think of bread today, but small cakes made with a mixture of barley flour, oil, and water, then flattened and baked on hot stones. It may not sound appetizing to us now, but it was then the everyday food of the common people.

BEANS, BROAD (pol); *Vicia faba.* 34″

The Hebrew word *pol* appears twice in the Bible, and there seems to be little doubt that it is correctly translated as "bean" or, more specifically, the "broad bean." Farmers still cultivate it, especially in Egypt. Archaeologists have discovered broad beans in some of the lower excavations of Jericho, and also in Egypt. People began to eat them early in China and throughout Asia. Though similar in many ways to the lima beans, they are not the same, for limas have a New World origin. Botanists have fairly well established that the wild progenitor of the broad bean has become extinct and that the present bean is not directly derived from any of the wild species of beans in the region.

Broad beans belong to the large family of legumes that includes not only the various species of beans, peas, lupins, peanuts, clovers, and vetches, but also a number of trees such as the locusts, mesquite, and acacias. These plants all have the ability to take nitrogen from the air and store it in root nodes, thus enriching the soil.

The broad bean was an important article of the diet for the Israelites. When David fled with his household from his son, Absalom, who had usurped the throne, Shobi, a loyal supporter, brought the unhappy royal party some of the comforts of life as well as food that included beans and lentils (2 Samuel 17:27-29). Most likely they were dried broad beans. People sometimes mixed them with barley, lentils, millet, and fitches, and ground them into flour for bread (Ezekiel 4:9). The Israelite housewife would cook the dried beans, as well as the young pods when still tender, and the mature but still unripe shelled beans. The term "pulse," as used in the Bible, may refer to beans, but it also included other garden herbs or vegetables.

CALAMUS—see Herbs and Spices

CANE—see Grass

CHICK PEA—see Pea, Chick

CORN—see Wheat, Barley, or Sorghum

COTTON (karpas); *Gossypium herbaceum. 36"*

The word *cotton* shows up only once in the Bible: Esther 1:6. At least one translation renders the Hebrew word *karpas* as "cotton." Most others translate it as "green" or omit it entirely. Apparently the passage should read as it does in the Revised Standard Version, "There were white cotton curtains and blue hangings," describing the glories of the palace of Ahasuerus in Shushan.

Farmers probably did not grow cotton in Palestine until after the return from Babylonian captivity, and the crop was apparently not important even then. Alexander the Great receives credit for introducing the short-stapled, coarse-fibered Asiatic cotton from northern India to Europe. It was not popular at first. Only the rich could afford it, and it did not seem to have any advantages over the fine linen that they already had. Egyptian cotton, a long-fibered high quality boll that is important today, actually originated in South and Central America. Important as cotton is in fabric manufacture throughout the world, people hardly knew of it during the biblical period.

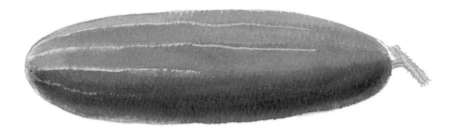

CUCUMBER (kishuim, mikshah); *Cucumis sativus.* 12"

Scholars tell us that our ordinary garden cucumber did not exist in Egypt as such during the early biblical period, and that it could not have been the one referred to in Numbers 11:5, where we find the children of Israel longing for some of the foods they had had in Egypt. The cucumber field mentioned in Isaiah 1:8 was a field of melons, as some of the more recent translations correctly portray it. The melons may have been a cylindrical, flat-tasting variety then widely grown there. Jeremiah 10:5 compares pagan idols to "scarecrows in a cucumber field" (RSV). The Authorized Version mentions cucumbers, in a marginal note, but the New International Version refers to it as a "melon patch," probably of the same type as cited above.

Our garden cucumbers originated in northern India, and they did eventually find their way to the Holy Land. We find, too, that the Romans were fond of them, and went to great pains to grow them indoors. The Emperor Tiberius allegedly had to have his cucumbers every day.

Whether or not the Romans were the ones to begin the practice of pickling them we can't be sure. As most gardeners know, cucumbers bear heavily in season, and we usually face the problem of using them up as fast as they come on. For that reason people sought ways of preserving them for the rest of the year. The long dark-green variety is the eating cucumber. Pickling cucumbers are usually smaller, more warty and prickly, and they are often also bitter when eaten raw. The bitterness disappears in the pickling process.

EMMER—see Wheat

FLAX (pishtah, pisheth) (linon); *Linum usitatissimum.* 24"

The early Egyptians planted large amounts of flax, and it was one of the crops badly damaged by the plague of hail that the Lord brought upon them before the Exodus (Exodus 9:31). The Egyptians made a high quality "fine linen" that they used for priestly robes and royal garments (Genesis 41:42; Exodus 28:39). The rich merchants of Tyre imported fine linen with "broidered work" from Egypt for the sails of their merchant ships. Mummies have linen wrappings that are equal in quality to what we make today.

Flax also grew in the hot and humid valley of the lower Jordan near the Dead Sea. Rahab, in Jericho, evidently worked in flax, for she hid Joshua's spies under bundles of flax drying on the rooftop (Joshua 2:6). The Bible mentions numerous uses for both the ordinary and the fine linen. The hangings of the tabernacle were of fine linen; Hannah brought her boy, Samuel, a linen garment yearly; Joseph of Arimathaea wrapped the body of Christ in linen after the Crucifixion. In Revelation 19:8 we read that the bride of the Lamb, the church, is to be "arrayed in fine linen," "for the fine linen is the righteousness of saints."

Bible translators are not sure of the use of the word silk in the Bible and feel that it should have been "fine linen" in most cases. In Revelation 18:12, however, they can be fairly certain that John intended silk, for he listed it with "fine linen." By that time silk had found its way into the economy and lexicon of Palestine.

The flax plant grows two to three feet tall, is slender, and has several light blue flowers on its branched tops. They mature into spherical capsules containing several flattened, slippery, brown seeds. During Bible times people fed most of the capsules to their livestock, but since then flax seeds have been found to contain a valuable drying oil employed in painting known as linseed oil. The seeds also are used as a laxative. The pulp left over from extracting the oil becomes feed for livestock.

In primitive times the farmer pulled the flax stalks up when mature and dried them. He removed the seed pods by stripping them off with a coarse comb. Then he soaked the stalks in water to rot the leaves and pulp. Another vigorous stripping combed off all the undesirable parts and left only the pale yellow fibers. The fibers were then spun into threads of unusual strength and durability. They went into nets, fishlines, cords, and cloth. Dusting with fuller's earth whitened the cloth.

GARBANZO—see Pea, Chick

GARLIC (shumin); *Allium sativum. 24"*

Only Numbers 11:5 speaks of garlic. "We remember the fish, which we did eat in Egypt freely; the cucumbers, and the melons, and the leeks, and the onions, and the garlick." Garlic developed in central Asia and received wide cultivation in Mediterranean countries as well. The Israelites apparently tired of the sweetish manna and longed for the pungent flavors of leeks, onions, and garlic, three members of the onion family that they had learned to enjoy in Egypt.

The garlic plant grows much like an onion except that the flower head sometimes has small bulbs instead of flowerets, and the bulb at the base divides into separate sections called cloves. A dry, papery covering that also encloses the whole bulb separates each clove or section. The grower propagates garlic by planting the individual cloves. Set in the ground in early spring, they mature in fall. The bulbs must be cured in the field, where they are hung in bunches by their braided stems. One may cut the cloves directly into food, or dry and grind them into powder.

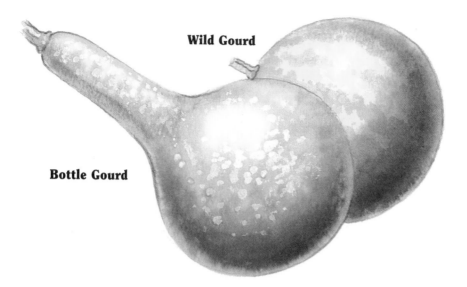

Wild Gourd

Bottle Gourd

GOURD, BOTTLE; calabash (kikajon, delaath, paqquoth, peqaim); *Lagenaria siceraria*

GOURD, WILD (pakouth-sadah); *Citrullus colocynthis.* 3″

In 1 Kings 6:18 and 7:24 we find references to *knops* (margin, "gourds") that the people used as decorative motifs in the interior embellishme.it of Solomon's Temple.

2 Kings 4:39-41 records a story involving the prophet Elisha. When he visited a School of the Prophets at Gilgal during a drought, one of the young men went out into the fields to find something to eat. He discovered a vine with gourds on it and came back with a lap full of them. Not knowing what they were, he shredded them into a pot, cooked them, and poured out helpings for the rest of them. As soon as the men tasted the gourds they exclaimed, "O thou man of God, there is death in the pot." Elisha put some meal in the pot, cooked the gourds a bit more, and they became edible. Some have contended that the "gourds" were poisonous mushrooms, but we have little ground for believing that, nor is there need to. Mushrooms do not thrive in the desert anyway.

The wild gourd is quite common in the hot deserts of southern Palestine and around Gilgal. It is able to survive in such inhospitable land by storing water in its perennial, thick roots which branch widely to draw moisture from the soil. From the short stem several long branches radiate, bearing deeply-cleft, watermelon-like leaves and yellow blossoms. The branches produce numerous, spherical, yellow, apple-sized fruits. Their hard shells are mottled with green, melon-like markings. The pulp is a powerful cathartic, widely used in small quantities as a medicine. In quantity it is a deadly poison. No wonder the sons of the Prophets became alarmed. When dried and ground up the seeds will make a coarse flour for use during famine.

The common bottle gourd of Palestine varies a lot in size and shape, but usually has a handle on a spherical body. The flesh is bitter, and in some varieties poisonous. Of African origin, the gourds have a wide distribution over that continent. The same species also inhabits South America, and scientists believe they floated across the ocean and propagated themselves in the New World much as coconuts do.

Bottle gourds are more useful as containers than as food. After one scoops the flesh out and dries the shell, it becomes a container or ladle. Egyptian tombs dated at 3500 B.C. have contained them, as well as some Peruvian and Mexican sites twice that old. Pumpkins and squash, such as we have now, are of American origin and would thus have been unknown in ancient Palestine. Muskmelons and watermelons were, however, a part of their diet.

The book of Jonah contains the story of how the Lord caused a gourd to grow miraculously in a day to shelter the prophet from the sun as he sat waiting for the destruction of Nineveh. Jonah appreciated the gourd, but when God caused a worm to destroy it, the prophet was extremely angry. The Lord sought by such an object lesson to teach Jonah to accept His mercy toward the repentant Ninevites.

Some have suggested that the gourd was probably a castor bean plant which grows rapidly and stands upright like a tree. Maybe it was, but it is not necessary for us to strain ourselves to rationalize the rapid growth. It was a plant that God created miraculously for the occasion, and there is probably no more point in trying to identify it than the big fish that God made to swallow Jonah shortly before this event.

GRASS (asab, chatsir, deshe, yereq, eseb, gez, achu) (chortos).

The numerous terms for grass in the Scriptures are usually rather general in nature and include a large number of herbaceous plants other than those in the Gramineae family. When Christ, in His sermon on the mount, said, "Wherefore, if God so clothe the grass of the field, which to day is, and to morrow is cast into the oven, shall he not much more clothe you, O ye of little faith?" (Matthew 6:30), He was referring to the whole carpet of grass, weeds, and flowers that covered the hillside on which He stood.

In this text, as in many others that mention the word, grass symbolizes ephemeral beauty, transience, and impermanence in contrast to the eternal verities of truth and love as exemplified in the kingdom of heaven.

In a land such as Palestine that has two seasons, the rainy and the dry, the fleeting nature of grass is more prominent than in countries where abundant rainfall keeps the grass green for a long time. In dry countries the grass comes up beautifully as the rains begin, but it soon shrivels and dies as the dry heat of summer arrives.

The arid range hills of the American West have a grass that sprouts thick and green in spring and gives promise of good pasture through the summer, but it quickly produces abundant seeds that mature and ripen as the rains end, and the grass dries up. The ranchers call it cheat grass because it promises and then fails to deliver. The cattle have to depend on the longer-lasting bunch grass that has a permanent root system and is accessible as dry feed even under the snows of winter.

Our text reminds us of a use for grass other than pasture or fodder. The clay ovens of a number of cultures used burning grass or straw to heat them. When they were hot, the housewife quickly cleaned out the ashes and placed loaves of bread inside. Then she closed the door. The heat remaining in the clay bricks was enough to bake the bread without additional fuel.

The Middle Eastern countries were the home of a number of cereal grasses such as wheat, barley, millet, and others. It was here that humanity first domesticated and grew them. We have dealt with a number of them under separate headings.

GRASS, GINGER—see Herbs and Spices

HOLLYHOCK; mallow (chalamuth); *Alcea setosa*; *Malva nicaeensis*. 60″

The KJV renders Job 6:6 as "Can that which is unsavoury be eaten without salt? or is there any taste in the white of an egg?" Other translations substitute "mallows" for "egg." In Job 30:4 we also read, "Who cut up mallows by the bushes, and juniper roots for their meat." The Hebrew word *chalamuth* can well be rendered as "mallow," the modern Hebrew for mallow being *halamith*. Several members of the mallow family, including the hollyhock, grow in Palestine. Not only are the large leaves used in soups and salads, but the unripe seed rings are not bad eating as I discovered when I was a boy.

Most mallows are biennial. The seedlings grow into a rosette of rounded leaves the first year, then the next spring a tall flower stalk shoots up. Both the hollyhock and the mallow have large, showy pink flowers that open up full to the sun and insects during the day, but close at night. When pollinated, they form a seed ring at the base of the petals formed by the carpels around the central style.

LEEK (hatzir, chatsir); *Allium porrum.* 18″

Leeks appear with onions and garlic as vegetables the Israelites longed for as a change from the sweetish manna they had been eating in the wilderness (Numbers 11:5). They are still widely cultivated in Egypt and Palestine and especially appreciated by the Jews.

Although closely related to the onions, leeks lack the enlarged bulb at the base. One plants them deep, heaping the earth up around the lower part of the plant so that part of the stem remains blanched. It swells a little and becomes the part of the plant that people usually eat, though the leaves of the young plants may go into stews and salads. Leeks have a milder taste than onions. People eat them both raw or cooked, but most of the time they use them to flavor foods. Often, however, cooks will prepare them with a white sauce and eat them on toast like asparagus.

Though of Middle Eastern origin, leeks early entered the cuisine of Italy when introduced by the Romans. Emperor Nero used to have them for several days every month to clear his voice. The Romans brought leeks to northern Europe, and they became so popular in Wales that the country adopted them as the national flower. Welshmen like to wear a sprig of leek in their hats on St. David's Day, March 1. In Scotland leeks became an important ingredient in their favorite Scotch winter broth. They are also an essential part of French cooking.

LENTIL (adashim); *Lens culinaris.* 12″

Lentils are the first of the legume, or pulse, vegetables to be mentioned in the Bible, and they are probably the first, according to archaeologists, to have been domesticated. Botanists believe that they originated in the Near East.

In Genesis 25:34 we read, "Then Jacob gave Esau bread and pottage of lentiles; and he did eat and drink, and rose up, and went on his way: thus Esau despised his birthright." Esau had come in from an unsuccessful hunt, faint with hunger, to find his brother stewing a pot of aromatic lentils over a fire. He asked for some, and Jacob, the hard bargainer, offered to give it to him for his birthright.

Lentils grow on a many-branched, vetch-type vine usually covered with small, pea-like, blue flowers. They mature into small pods, each of which contains only one seed, but a single vine may have a hundred pods. The seeds consist of two halves that separate during threshing. The flattened seed halves may be either yellow, brick red, or gray. Lentils grow on light soil and are sometimes thought of as the food of the poor, but they are highly nutritious and make good soups, stews, and pastes rich in protein and carbohydrates. The vines provide excellent fodder for sheep and cattle.

The Hebrew *adashim* appears four times in the Bible, and there seems to be little doubt about its translation as lentils. Ezekiel 4:9 lists lentils as one of the ingredients of a multiple grain bread that God instructed the prophet to make.

MALLOW—see Hollyhock

MANDRAKE—see Herbs and Spices

MILLET (dochan); *Panicum miliaceum.* 40″

The passage in Ezekiel 4:9 naming the ingredients of the bread God commanded the prophet to bake, contains the only appearance in the Bible of the Hebrew word *dochan*, correctly translated as "millet." Scholars have little doubt that the Israelites used millet—in fact, they may have grown more than one variety. Mankind domesticated it from the wild millet of Ethiopia early in human history, and archaeologists have found it in a number of ancient Mesopotamian digs.

Millet is a grass bearing heavy panicles of small seeds, or, in the case of the foxtail types, heavy, rounded racemes. Palestinian farmers grew it as a summer crop requiring irrigation. For that reason it was not as popular as wheat or barley, which matured before the dry season arrived. The people ground millet into a coarse flour for cakes and also used it as animal feed. The stalks, after threshing, were made into brooms.

In the United States we sow millet as a grass, also as grain feed for poultry and cattle, and to supply the many bird-feeding stations around the country with the bulk of commercial birdseed. However, only a few of the smaller birds eat it. India raises more millet than most other countries of the world, and the grain feeds almost one third of the world's peasant population. It is sometimes referred to as the poor man's cereal because it can grow on poor soils where other crops do not bear as well.

MUSKMELON (kishuim, mikshah); *Cucumis melo*.

People apparently first domesticated muskmelons in what is now Iran, but more than 20 species of them grow in eastern Africa and it is quite possible that some of the kinds came from there. One melon of a long, cylindrical shape raised in Egypt may have been the "cucumber" referred to by the Israelites (Numbers 11:5) as one of the foods they longed for in the wilderness. We know that cucumbers such as we have today did not exist in Egypt at that early time. Melons they did have.

Muskmelons, as most gardeners know, cross easily with other species, and the resulting products are in most cases inferior to the originals. This makes it important to keep pure species at some distance from other varieties of melons so they will not cross-pollinate. They do not, however, cross with watermelons, squash, or cucumbers, since they are in a different genus. Because of this ready crossing the taste and appearance of muskmelons may vary widely. They may be deep-fleshed, orange, and sweet, or have shallow, pale flesh that is absolutely flat in taste. Most of the melons grown in Bible times were a far cry from the typical netted-skinned, uniform cantaloupes we find in our supermarkets. Even the ones in stores are not nearly as good tasting and aromatic as they could be, for growers now are more concerned with shelf life than flavor of fruits and vegetables.

We may be sure that some of the melons grown then had good flavors, because we read in Isaiah 1:8 of "a lodge in a garden of cucumbers [melons]." It is hard to visualize having someone living in a cucumber field to guard such vegetables, but if they were melons, it is more plausible. Even in the United States more than one farmer has had to watch a watermelon patch with a shotgun when they were ripening. In addition to the smooth-skinned, yellow muskmelons, the Israelites probably also grew the large casabas, Persian melons, and possibly honeydews and others to delight their appetites.

ONION (batzal); *Allium cepa.* 30″

Only the passage where the Israelites long for certain foods of Egypt (Numbers 11:5) alludes to the onion. They doubtless ate their onions raw, both the bulb and the stalk, but they also used them to season their broths and soups.

Originating in central Asia, onion culture quickly spread in ancient times over most of the known world. In time a large, mild onion known as the Egyptian developed. We now have many varieties noted for their sweetness or mildness as well as the varying degrees of offensiveness of flavor or odor. Their stronger flavors result from a highly volatile oil that spreads into the air as one cuts or peels the onion. The oil stings the eyes and causes the tears to flow copiously.

The onion is a member of the amaryllis group in the lily family. It is a biennial, growing a cluster of leaves and a bulb the first year from a planted seed. The next year, if one plants or leaves the bulb in the ground, it grows a tall, hollow stem with a swelling about a third of the way down. At the top of the stem a ball-like seed head forms. On some varieties small onions form the head instead of florets and seeds. The grower can plant the small onions. Most home gardeners raise their onions from "sets," small immature onion bulbs kept over from the previous year. They rapidly produce green leaves for eating, and then mature into full-sized bulbs by fall.

PEA, CHICK; garbanzo (hamitz); *Cicer arietinum*. 16"

Isaiah 30:24 states: "The oxen likewise and the young asses that ear the ground shall eat clean provender, which hath been winnowed with the shovel and with the fan." The prophet here describes the prosperity and plenty that would come to Israel should they return to serving the Lord. Even the lowly oxen and asses that "ear," or "till," the soil, ordinarily fed only barley mixed with straw, would have "clean provender," mixed fodder or mash, to eat. The Hebrew *hamitz* actually refers to chick peas and should have been translated as that instead of "provender."

The chick pea, or garbanzo, has always had wide cultivation in the Mediterranean countries, being domesticated from wild species that still grow in Asia Minor. It has shown up in archaeological digs in Turkey that date back to 5000 B.C.

The plant is a leafy bush, covered with hairy leaflets that usually feel damp to the picker. The pods are small, and each contains only one or two of the small, rounded peas. The shape of the pea, with the projecting germ on one side, has the appearance of a chick's head and beak, accounting for the name.

Another plant in the pulse group that we are better acquainted with is the ordinary garden pea. It was also domesticated in Bible lands from wild species that still grow there, and though widely grown in early times as now, Scripture never mentions it.

RIE—see Wheat

SORGHUM (durrah); *Sorghum bicolor.* 60"

While not actually spoken of in Scripture, the Bible might have lumped sorghum with the millet. It grows in Palestine now, is well suited to the climate, and evidence indicates that it existed there during the biblical period. The plant is quite tall, like corn, but the leaves are narrower and the top has a dense panicle of seeds, making it suitable for livestock feed. One can also make the hulled seeds into a coarse flour for cakes. Farmers in the United Sates raise sorghum in four varieties: for grain, sugar cane, fodder, and broom corn.

SPELT—see Wheat

WATERMELON—see Muskmelon

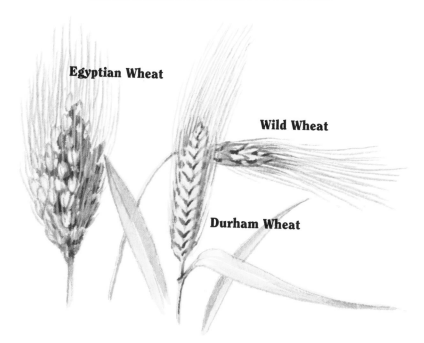

Egyptian Wheat

Wild Wheat

Durham Wheat

WHEAT, DURUM (chittah, chintah) (sitos); *Triticum durum.* 36″

WHEAT, EMMER (kussemeth, kussemoth, kussmim); *Triticum dicoccum* (also bar, dagan, kama, avur, omer, geresh, carmel).

WHEAT, WILD; *triticum dicoccoides.*

Wheat, the most important cereal crop in the world today, also held that role in the Biblical world. Early in human history man domesticated the grain from the wild wheat that grew in Palestine as well as in Mesopotamia and Syria. Wild wheat had short ears that disintegrated easily as the grain ripened and scattered its grains irregularly on the ground. The small kernels had tight hulls that would not come off easily.

Emmer wheat developed from the wild variety. Its ears held together better, but the hulls were still hard to remove. The new wheat grew on land that was poor and dry, and for that reason people raised it extensively even in New Testament times to make a coarse flour and grits. The New International Version refers to it as *spelt* in Exodus 9:32, Isaiah 28:25, and Ezekiel 4:9, but spelt is a central European wheat, unknown in Palestine. The KJV renders it as "rie," but such a translation is also doubtful because rye, *Secale cereale*, is a cold climate grain grown largely in northern European countries. It contains less gluten than wheat flour, and bread made from it usually turns out heavy and dark. Palestinian farmers did not raise it.

When durum wheat developed in very early times (two varieties appear in archaeological sites in Iraq dated at 6700 B.C.) it soon took precedence over emmer. It was a hard wheat with longer, less brittle ears than emmer, and hulls that separated easily from the kernels. The Hebrew *chittah* refers specifically to it. The KJV translates *chittah* 70 times as "corn" and 30 as "wheat." *Corn* is, of course, the older English term referring to grain in general, or more specifically, wheat in England and oats in Scotland and Ireland. What North Americans call corn has a New World origin and that use of the word had not yet entered the vocabulary of the Bible translators. To avoid confusion the New World grain should have been called maize.

Egypt had still another variety of wheat, *Triticum compositum*, that bore several heads clumped together on one stem. It is, no doubt, what Pharaoh saw in his dream (Genesis 41:22): "seven ears came up in one stalk, full and good," followed by seven "blasted" ears that represented the seven future years of famine.

Farmers in Palestine grow wheat in the fall. When the "early rains" came, the moisture softened the ground so that the farmer could plow and harrow it. Then they sowed the wheat. A common way is often pictured in connection with the parable of the sower. The farmer holds the grain in a bag in the crook of one arm, and with the other he scatters the seeds with a flip motion of his hand as he walks back and forth over the field. A good workman can distribute the grain quite evenly, but it is inevitable that some of it should fall on hard ground, stony places, or among thistles, as in Christ's parable.

Besides the broadcast method, ancient farmers also sometimes planted wheat in rows. Archaeologists have unearthed plows that included a hopper and a spout that evenly dropped the seed into the earth behind the plowshare. With such a combination plow/seeder the farmer could sow his grain in rows as he plowed and be sure that it was properly covered.

In late fall the heavy rains come, and the wheat sprouts and forms a good root system and green basal leaves. Then in spring, as the sun warms the ground, the stalks shoot up quickly. As they head out, the "latter rain" matures the wheat before it ripens. Then the rains end and the villagers harvest and thresh the crop. As Proverbs 26:1 indicates, the farmers realized the problems of "rain in harvest."

The Bible mentions threshing and threshing floors a number of times. The threshing floor was often communal. It was situated on a hilltop or open place to take advantage of a breeze. The floor itself was a level enclosure of hardened earth or of stones and mortar. On it the farmer laid the stalks of grain after drying. Then, if the operation was small, the husbandman used a flail to beat the grains out of the ears. It was a wooden rod about three or four feet long, with a shorter piece of hardwood tied to it by a leather thong. With this the thresher beat the stalks until he had freed all the kernels from the hulls.

If the threshing operation was more than he could handle with a flail, the farmer spread the grain over the floor and a team of oxen pulled a wooden sled with a man on it over the cut grain, rubbing out the kernels and reducing the straw to chaff. Still another alternative was to drive a cart with heavy wheels over the grain. Oxen or donkeys hauled it in circles until it had reduced the grain to straw and separated the kernels. The thresher then forked or raked off the straw and kept it for feed. The grain and chaff he swept together in a pile to winnow.

Winnowing was done by tossing the grain and chaff into the air with a basin or shovel in a light breeze. The breeze blew away the chaff and dust, leaving the heavier grain to fall back to the ground. The threshers then fanned the floor (Matthew 3:12) and gathered up all the precious grain and stored it in earthen jars or mouseproof bins in storehouses. The farmer fed the chaff to the stock or burned it in the ovens for baking.

Long before people even thought of making yeast-risen bread from wheat flour, they ground the grain into coarse grits and cooked it as porridge. They still do this today. When people began to cultivate the hard durum wheat, they found that the flour made from it had a high gluten content that made the bread rise, especially when they added yeast to it and kneaded the dough.

Grinding stones gradually improved. In the more primitive types the "nether" stone was saddle-shaped and rectangular. The upper stone was smaller, and the operator rubbed it back and forth on the bottom stone with the grain in between. It must have been one of these that a certain woman, as recorded in Judges 9:53, cast "upon Abimelech's head . . . to brake his skull."

In the rotating mill both stones were circular, about eighteen inches in diameter and about three inches thick. The lower one was slightly convex with a wooden peg set in the center. The upper one was slightly concave underneath and had a hole in the center large enough to allow it to rotate on the central wooden peg and also to accommodate the grain poured into it. It had one or two pegs mounted near the outer edge by which the operator could move it either in a semicircular motion or rotation. Usually one or two women sat on the ground beside it as they worked it. The ground meal sifted out from the edges of the stones to fall on the cloth or goat skin underneath them.

The noise of the grinding wheels was a common one in Biblical villages, and was a comforting sound for it meant that the village had grain available as food. In Ecclesiastes 12:3, 4 we read, "and the grinders [shall] cease because they are few, . . . when the sound of grinding is low." Jesus, speaking of His second coming, declared, "Two women shall be grinding at the mill; the one shall be taken, and the other left" (Matthew 24:41). Both texts evidently refer to this type of mill.

Larger mills also came into use. Basically they followed the same principle as the above, but on a greater scale. The upper stone had a pole or rods fastened to it, and a donkey or slave walking in a circle around it turned the millstone. Samson worked such a mill after the Philistines captured and blinded him (Judges 16:21). A passage in Lamentations 5:13 alludes to it: "They took the young men to grind." The angel in Revelation 18:21 probably threw a boulder into the sea the size of "a great millstone" such as this.

Millstones of necessity consisted of hard volcanic stone that would not grind up with the grain itself. We find reference to that in Job 41:24 where God uses the simile of the heart of the crocodile being as hard as the "nether millstone."

Wheat became an important cereal crop of the Romans. Excavations of the city of Pompeii discovered a bakery that had three large grinding mills in the courtyard and 80 loaves of bread in the ovens.

The ancients greatly feared crop failures and as a preventative measure the Romans celebrated a spring festival at which they sacrificed a red dog. Today the Festival of St. Mark occurs on the same day, April 25, and people offer prayers for the crops.

The early and the latter rains were not always dependable in Palestine, and if they did not come, as often happened, the grain did not mature and famine resulted. In such times Egypt often still had food, because farming in the Nile valley depended on irrigation, not rain. In addition the people could store the more bountiful harvests as Joseph did before the seven lean years (Genesis 42).

In Palestine some of the best wheatlands were the coastal plains occupied by the Philistines. Samson destroyed some of their ripening crops by turning loose his 300 "foxes" into the fields with firebrands tied between their tails (Judges 15:4, 5). At a later time they had plagues of mice in their fields as a result of keeping the captured ark of the Israelites (1 Samuel 6:5). We find too that the Midianites allowed the Israelites to grow their grain, then they seized it during harvest. That was why Gideon threshed his wheat in secret in the winepress instead of on the threshing floor (Judges 6:3-11).

When Jesus and His disciples "threshed corn" on the Sabbath (Matthew 12:1-5), they were plucking the ripe heads of wheat in the field, rubbing out the kernels in their palms, and eating them. I remember doing the same thing as a boy. The fresh wheat had a pleasant taste, and the kernels were not nearly as hard as they are after drying thoroughly. The kernels of wheat in Bible times were smaller than ours, and they had a slightly bitter aftertaste, but they were still a tasty snack to allay hunger. We sometimes chew the kernels without swallowing them, and the gluten would form into a wad of "chewing gum" in our mouths, a property utilized today in many of the gluten products made from wheat.

A number of parables in the Bible deal with the sowing and harvesting of wheat. Best known, probably, though it does not specifically name the grain as wheat, is the one about the sower and the seed found in Matthew 13:1-23. The good seed in the parable bore thirty-, sixty-, and a hundred-fold, meaning that many kernels resulted from one original seed. Usually several stems come up from one stalk, and the ears on the stems may have had 15 to 20 kernels. Today the average would be nearer 50. I have heard the increase in the parable interpreted as 30, 60, or 100 bushels to the acre, speaking in American farmer's terms. If he sowed one and a half bushels to the acre, it would come to somewhere near the same amounts, but that is not exactly the term that Christ had in mind then.

Another parable follows in verses 24-30. In it the husbandman sowed clean wheat in his field; but while he slept an enemy came and sowed tares (darnel or Syrian scabious). When both came up, the servants wanted to pull up the tares, but the master told the men to leave them together till the harvest, then throw the tares into the fire and burn them, thus avoiding damage to the roots of the wheat.

Matthew 3:12 quotes John the Baptist referring to Christ as coming with a fan to the threshing floor to purge the wheat and gather it into His storehouse, and "burn up the chaff with unquenchable fire."

Jesus, in John 12:24, calls attention to the fact that a kernel of wheat that falls into the ground must die before it can bring forth fruit. In another parable Jesus spoke of the selfish rich man whose bumper crops would not fit into his storehouses. He decided to build greater ones so he could enjoy all his riches for himself and be secure for his whole future; but that night he died without being able to enjoy any of his bounty (Luke 12:16-23).

Herbs and Spices

Apparently herbs and spices had great importance to the people of the Bible world, and Scripture mentions a large number of them, so we are grouping them together here.

Among the medicinal plants a number have demonstrated healing properties, but many of them were prescribed and used just because they smelled vile and tasted bitter and strong. Some produced violent reactions and narcotic effects, and a number were actually poisonous in large enough doses.

Many of the plants in our list provided flavoring in food, and considering the monotony of the coarse fare of the common people, it is understandable that the ancients would want to add something to improve the taste. Quite a number of the herbs were cooked and eaten, and some were used raw as salad.

A large number of plants attracted attention because of their pleasant odor. They found use as perfumes and deodorants to counteract the too-fragrant body odors of the "great unwashed" that included even the rich. Millenniums would pass before the daily bath rendered them unnecessary, only to be replaced by a myriad of concoctions that commerce today foists upon us by high-pressure, extravagantly expensive advertising. We can judge the importance of some of the aromatic herbs and spices to the people of that time from the fact that well established trade routes existed from Ethiopia, Egypt, and Rome to far away India and China. Palestine, situated at the crossroads of some of the important routes, profited by it.

ALOE (ahaloth [?]) (aloe); *Aloe vera.* 16″

Though the Scriptures mention the aloe a number of times, in almost every case scholars believe that it is the eaglewood tree that the Bible writer intends. For that reason most of the references to it here will be found under that head. However, the New Testament text (John 19:39, 40) that tells of Nicodemus bringing a 100-pound mixture of myrrh and aloes preparatory to the burial of Jesus, most likely does refer to the aloe.

A small, succulent plant with a rosette of tapered, thorn-edged, fleshy leaves, it grows throughout much of the Near East. People widely used it as a medicine and also for embalming purposes. It seems quite plausible that Nicodemus would have brought some of it for embalming the body of Jesus.

The plant looks much like the American century plant, or agave, but the latter is not closely related for the aloe belongs to the Liliaceae family and the agave to the Amaryllidaceae family. In a broad sense, however, they are both lilies. The aloe vera is presently undergoing a resurgence of popularity as a medical cure-all.

ANISE—see Dill

BITTER HERBS (merorim).

CHICORY, DWARF; *Cichorium pumilum.* 30″
REICHARDIA; *Reichardia tingitana.* 10″

In the preparation of the Passover meal the Israelites had instructions from God to eat the Passover lamb "roasted; with unleavened bread and bitter herbs" (Exodus 12:8, RSV). The bitter herbs consisted of chicory, endive, lettuce, and watercress. The chicory was identical to the European weed by that name which has become common along our country roads and alleys. We also have a cultivated variety that is quite similar. The light blue flowers bloom in midsummer, but one can pick the rather coarse, oblong leaves with a prominent mid-rib much earlier when they are still tender and use them as a food seasoning and as greens. Their tartness adds a little zest to the food.

By drying, grinding, and roasting the root of the chicory, one can make it into a coffee substitute. People often used it to adulterate real coffee, a practice that stopped with the adoption of pure food laws.

Another plant that we could include with bitter herbs was the reichardia. This desert plant is similar to our common dandelion. It grows a rosette of pale green, dentate leaves from which rise hollow stems with yellow ray flowers on them. People gather the green leaves in early spring, as we gather dandelion greens, and cook them with their meals or eat them as a salad. The flowers mature into puffball seed heads from which the achenes scatter in the breeze.

CALAMAS—see Ginger

CASSIA; Chinese ginger (qiddah, qesiah, ketziah, kiddah); *Cinnamomun cassia.* 30'

The Old Testament refers to cassia as one of the ingredients of the perfumes used to anoint various objects in the tabernacle ceremonies (Exodus 30:24). In Psalm 45 we read, "All thy garments smell of myrrh, and aloes, and cassia" (verse 8). Ezekiel 27:19 refers to it as a trade item among the eastern nations. It was not native to Palestine, but came from India and China.

This perfume and spice derives from the bark, leaves, and twigs of the Chinese cinnamon tree that grows to be around 30 feet tall. Its manufacturers obtain the perfume as oil by steam distillation. The spice comes from the dried inner bark and can be ground and used in seasoning sweetmeats and wine. The taste is supposed to be similar to the real cinnamon, but more pungent and less delicate in flavor. The Chinese cinnamon, because it is more common and has a thicker bark, is cheaper than the real, and is often substituted for the Ceylonese cinnamon. People in Bible times apparently knew both, since the Scriptures mention both cassia and cinnamon.

CASTOR BEAN (kikayum); *Ricinus communis.* 15′

The Hebrew *kikayon* appears in the Bible only in the book of Jonah, and translators have treated it in various ways. In the Authorized Version it is "gourd," in the New International Version it is "vine," and in some others it is just "plant." An alternative choice of "castor bean" has been suggested for various reasons. The Greek historian Herodotus mentions *kaka* as a plant grown widely in Egypt and surrounding areas for its oil. The Talmud refers to *kikayon* as a medicinal plant from which castor oil was extracted even in early times.

The story in Jonah states that the plant grew rapidly and shaded the prophet from the sun. A gourd would lie on the ground unless it already had a framework to climb on. The castor bean is a large, erect plant that can reach 15 to 20 feet tall in a short time, even 30 feet in a good environment. It has abundant, large, palmate leaves that can supply cooling shade. It is, however, not woody and will collapse after frost or worm damage, as the account suggests. But at the same time we should remember that the text says, "The Lord prepared a [gourd, vine, or whatever]." So it may not have been any known species any more than the creature that swallowed Jonah. For the plant to grow that large in a day required a bona fide miracle anyway.

The castor bean is a native of the Middle Eastern countries, and dense stands of it grow in the canyons and river valleys. It produces clusters of bristly seed capsules that enclose large, beautifully marked "beans." While they are called beans, the plant is not a bean, but a member of the spurge family. The leaves and fruit contain a deadly poison known as "ricinine," but the oil expressed from the seeds has long served as a laxative. Also one can use it as a lubricant in boat and airplane engines because it remains thick through a wide range of temperatures.

CHICORY—see Bitter Herbs

CINNAMON, CEYLON (qinnamon) (kinnamomon); *Cinnamomon zeylanicum.* 25'

The genuine cinnamon tree is a little smaller than the Chinese cinnamon, or cassia. Both belong to the laurel family and have leathery, oblong, evergreen leaves placed opposite each other on the twigs. The thin, reddish bark has a spicy taste. Growing on the Island of Sri Lanka and surrounding areas, it is the cinnamon identified with the Hebrew *qinnamon* mentioned several times in the Scriptures. In Exodus 30:23 God instructed Moses regarding the details of the sanctuary service: "Take thou also unto thee principal spices, of pure myrrh five hundred shekels, and of sweet cinnamon half so much." We can be sure that it was not cassia, because the next verse lists cassia as an additional spice.

Proverbs 7:17 gives cinnamon as one of the spices that the harlot used to prepare her bed. Revelation 18:13 includes it with all the precious and costly merchandise that the fallen Babylon has had as her stock in trade. Well established trade routes linked Palestine to China, India, southern Arabia, and Egypt in ancient times. Thus the people of Palestine knew about such exotic trade items as cinnamon.

CINNAMON, CHINESE—see Cassia

CORIANDER (gad, gidda); *Coriandrum sativum*. 36"

Coriander appears in the KJV of Exodus 16:31 and Numbers 11:7. Both instances include it as part of the description of manna: "it was like coriander seed, white; and the taste of it was like wafers made with honey." Numbers adds, "the colour thereof as the colour of bdellium."

We have some reason to doubt whether the right plant is named here, for coriander does not grow in the Sinai desert, though the Israelites might have known it from Egypt. In addition, the color of coriander seed is not white, but a brownish tan. The color of bdellium may be closer, but we do not know exactly what it is. If it is a resinous amber, it may have had some of the brownish tints and was probably translucent. The Arabian cognate *gidda* refers to *Artemisia*, or wormwood, a plant related to our sagebrush. A number of other desert plants have seeds that more resemble the appearance of manna.

Like dill, coriander belongs to the carrot family. It reaches about three feet tall, has finely divided leaves—also like dill—and its flowers and fruits grow in umbels. The seeds are more globular, but much the same size as dill or carrot seeds. They have a sweetish, pleasant taste, and people use them in flavoring food. One can express an aromatic oil from them. If manna was no larger than a coriander seed, it would have meant a good, long day's work for an Israelite to pick an omer of it off the ground and not have a lot of sand in it.

CRESS, WATER—see Bitter Herbs

CROCUS, SAFFRON (karkom); *Crocus sativus.* 5″

Saffron appears only in Songs of Solomon 4:14, where it forms part of a list of ointments and perfumes used by the spouse in the poem. Scholars think it is derived from the saffron crocus, a low-growing flower with grasslike leaves and lavender blue blossoms that have yellow stigmas. It is the familiar crocus widely planted in lawns and flower beds and usually the first flower to bloom in spring.

People collected the stigmas and made them into perfume, medicine, or a yellow dye. It took a lot of picking to get enough to do any amount of dyeing. This crocus, which may also have yellow blossoms, did not grow in Palestine during early Bible times, and its trade was limited to kings or wealthy individuals. Later it was introduced and planted.

Another plant that may have been referred to as saffron is the turmeric. Still sold in Arab markets as *kurkum,* it serves as a spice and medicine. Indian turmeric, *Curcuma longa,* is a tall plant of the ginger family that rises from fleshy underground rhizomes. These roots are yellow-orange to brown inside and, when boiled, dried, and ground, yield an orange-yellow powder widely used in southern Asia as curry powder for food flavoring and coloring, also for dyeing cloth. The saffron robes of the priests obtained their color from turmeric. Turmeric does not grow in Palestine, but it could well have been a trade item during the Biblical period.

Still another plant that may have been called saffron is the safflower, *Carthamus tinctorius*, a thistlelike annual in the sunflower family that also provides a yellow dye. Grown in Egypt and Palestine, it would have been available to the people of that time. Today we make a low cholesterol cooking oil from its seeds.

CUMMIN (camon, kammon) (kuminon); *Cuminum cyminum.* 12″

Christ refers to cummin in Matthew 23:23 in connection with mint and dill as one of the herbs that the Pharisees tithed meticulously at the expense of more important values such as justice, mercy, and faith. Isaiah 28:25-27 describes it as being sown broadcast and threshed with a rod rather than a flail.

This herb is similar to dill in that it has small, white flowers arranged in umbels, and that it belongs to the carrot family. The seeds look like those of dill and have a strong aromatic smell to them. They have a warm, bitter taste, hotter than caraway seeds, but appreciated in the Middle Eastern countries that grow it extensively. Cooks use it as a food spice in India and Mexico as well as the Mediterranean countries, and it also provides a perfume and an antidote for spasms.

The cummin plant is slender and branching. It grows to about a foot in height and its leaves are finely divided as are those of dill and several of the other umbelliferae.

CUMMIN, BLACK; nutmeg flower; fennelflower (ketzaeh); *Nigella sativa.* 36″

In Isaiah 28:27 we read, "For the fitches are not threshed with a threshing instrument, neither is the cart wheel turned about upon the cummin; but the fitches are beaten out with a staff, and the cummin with a rod." The RSV substitutes "dill" for "fitches." Scholars now believe that neither one is correct. It should read "black cummin" instead. Both the black cummin and the ordinary cummin have small seeds, many of which would be lost on the threshing floor or when ground under the cart wheel. Instead, the harvester lays the dried plants on a cloth or goatskin and beats them by hand, the black cummin with a staff because it has the larger pods, and the other cummin with a smaller rod, for that is all that it takes to release the seeds from the umbels.

Black cummin, fennelflower, or nutmeg flower, as it is variously called, is an annual herb about three feet tall with finely divided leaves like dill and cummin. Here the resemblance ceases, since the black cummin does not have an umbel with flowers and seeds, but large, showy yellow or blue, five-petaled flowers instead, with numerous stamens. The many small, black seeds develop in angular capsules that have six or seven horns on top.

Present-day Arabs and Jews still follow the custom of sprinkling black cummin seed over their bread or cakes, and they use them also to flavor some of their other dishes.

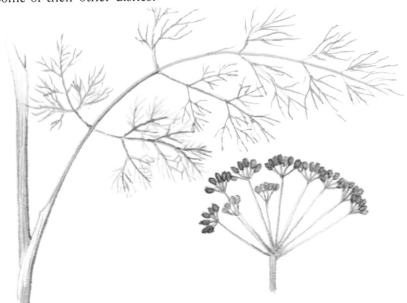

DILL (qetsach, sheveth) (anethon); *Anethum graveolens* 24"

The KJV translates the Greek *anethon* as anise. Anise is, however, a plant of European culture, and it is doubtful whether anyone ever grew it in Palestine. For that reason many believe that it should have been translated as "dill" instead. The instruction in the Mishnah regarding tithing of plants, seeds, and pods does refer to dill. The one reference in the Scripture is Matthew 23:23, where Christ reprimands the Pharisees for being so strict in the tithing of dill, mint, and cummin, but neglecting weightier matters such as justice, mercy, and faith.

The Hebrew *etsach*, as used in Isaiah 28:25, 27, has been translated as dill or fitches. It could also have been black cummin, or fennelflower, *Nigella sativa*, a member of the crowfoot family.

Dill is a common garden herb about two feet tall. It belongs to the carrot family and like most others of that group, it has large umbels of greenish-white flowers and foliage minutely divided into threadlike lobes. The flowers mature into aromatic seeds that will flavor food and also, medicinally, relieve gas on the stomach. The green leaves are used in pickling cucumbers—dill pickles.

EAGLEWOOD (ahaloth) (agallochon, xylalve); *Aquilaria agallocha.* 100'

Most scholars believe that the aloe of the Bible is more likely the product of the eaglewood tree of East Africa and India than the aloe vera plant. The eaglewood is a tall tree with aromatic wood and leaves. It has entire, alternate leaves, clusters of colored flowers, and bivalved seed capsules. The trees belong to the Thymelaeaceae family, of which the aromatic thyme of our spice shelves is also a member. Botanists recognize some 20 species of the trees.

During Balaam's prophecy of Israel's future (Numbers 24:6) he refers to "trees of lign aloes which the Lord hath planted." His statement makes it appear that they may have been native to Palestine. They were also important, among other perfumes and spices, in Israel's trade with surrounding nations.

The uses of aloes in the Bible records seem to be as a fragrant perfume: "Thy garments smell of myrrh, and aloes, and cassia" (Psalm 45:8); "I have perfumed my bed with . . . aloes" (Proverbs 7:17); and "Thy plants are an orchard . . . of frankincense; myrrh and aloes" (Song of Solomon 4:13, 14). This characteristic of perfume seems to fit the eaglewood better than the aloe vera.

In the case of Nicodemus and the 100-pound mixture of myrrh and aloes that he brought for the burial of Jesus, it could have been either chips of eaglewood or a solution of aloes.

ENDIVE—see Bitter Herbs

FITCHES—see Cummin, Black

FRANKINCENSE (lebona, levona) (libanos); *Boswellia sacra.* 75'

The Bible speaks of frankincense in connection with the sanctuary and Temple services (Exodus 30:34, 35), and also as one of the gifts brought to the Christ Child by the Magi (Matthew 2:10, 11). It is the dried gum of several trees and shrubs of the genus *Boswellia* in the Burseraceae family which also includes the elephant trees of northern Mexico. They grew in areas south of Palestine. Boswellia trees have pinnate leaves and small, greenish-white flowers. The gum drips from cuts and bruises in the bark, and people collect it after it has dried. In Bible times it was an important article of commerce carried by Arab traders as well as Phoenician sailors from southern Arabia and India to Palestine and Europe. People used it not only as incense, but as something to cure almost any kind of ailment, including leprosy. Today scientists regard it as having no medical value at all.

Deep cuts made in the bark of the trunk and branches of the trees will increase production. Then the gum collectors will peel away the outside bark below the cut to allow a clean place for it to gather. The milky juice drips down like thick tears and hardens on contact with the air. In about three months, when it reaches a workable consistency, the Arabs scrape it off into baskets, pack it in goatskins, and transport it by camel to the markets. The gum is whitish on the surface, but almost colorless inside when pure. One refines it by dissolving it in alcohol and filtering it. When burned, it gives off the desirable incense for which the ancients prized it. Some churches still use it in their services.

GALBANUM (helbenah, chelbenah); *Ferula gummosa.* 40″

Exodus 30:34 and Ecclesiasticus 24:14, 15 mention this component of incense and perfume as a spice employed in the temple and by royalty. Though its identity is not absolutely certain, the term *galbanum* seems to refer to the gum exuding from the *Ferula gumosa* plant, a tall herb in the carrot family that did not grow in Palestine, but in Iran, Afghanistan, and India. The Jews imported it with other exotic spices. If it is Ferula gummosa gum, it has a rather fetid, musky odor and a bitter taste to our present-day taste buds.

The spice collectors produce the gum by cutting into the plant a few inches above the ground and allowing the sap to flow and congeal in a yellow-brownish mass that they gather and sell.

The ferula plant reaches three to four feet tall and has a fairly heavy stem along with sturdy branches and profusely divided leaves. At the top it branches into several stems bearing umbels of yellowish flowers.

The Greeks ascribed great healing powers to the galbanum gum, but modern medicine has found little to support such a belief.

GINGER; *Zingiber officianale.*

GINGER GRASS (kaneh, kaneh hatov, knei-bosem); *Cymbopogon martinii.* 12"

The Israelites used a number of aromatic grasses, referring to them as "aromatic cane" in Exodus 30:23, RSV; as "sweet cane" in Jeremiah 6:20, RSV; and as "calamas" in Ezekiel 27:19-21, RSV. "Sweet calamus" was another term for ginger grass.

The spice we know as ginger is yet another grasslike plant that the Greeks and Romans imported from southern Arabia and India. It is native to the warmer portions of Asia, but people have planted and widely cultivated it over much of the tropical world today. It grows from rhizomes, which, when bleached, dried, and ground, yield the ginger of commerce. Our American wild ginger, *Asarum canadense*, is quite distinct from the ones we have mentioned both in botanical family and appearance, but its root also contains a stimulant, and one can use it as a spice.

People in Bible times employed ginger grass, or calamus, as a perfume, cosmetic, flavoring, and medicine. Steaming would distill aromatic oils from it. When archaeologists first opened some of the old Egyptian tombs in modern times, the sweet aroma of camel grass, another variety, was still perceptible. Still another aromatic grass, lemon grass, was also in common use. One can distill oil from these grasses, and each one is distinct chemically and in aroma from the others in the group.

GRASS, CAMEL — see Ginger

HEMLOCK, POISON (rosh); *Conium maculatum.* 5"

The precise word for poison hemlock does not appear in the Bible, but scholars think that the Hebrew *rosh,* translated as gall and poison, may have originally referred to hemlock and then has taken on the general meaning of poison. Scripture usually associates poison with serpents, but sometimes the term involves plant poison as in the case of the pot of gourds in 2 Kings 4:39, 40.

Lamentations 3:19 ("Remembering mine affliction and my misery, the wormwood and the gall") connects gall with another plant, indicating that it also had a plant origin. The passages involving gall most familiar to us are those dealing with the crucifixion: "They gave him vinegar to drink mingled with gall: and when he had tasted thereof, he would not drink" (Matthew 27:34). Some commentators think that gall in this case may have been poison hemlock.

Poison hemlock, an herb belonging to the carrot family, grows two to six feet tall from a heavy taproot. It has a dense foliage of finely divided leaves the first year. The next year a stout stem rises, topped with umbels of small white flowers. People sometimes mistake the lush, green foliage for parsley and eat it with disastrous results. It has a disagreeable odor. Children sometimes get poisoned when they make whistles out of its hollow stems. The seeds resemble dill, but they are also poisonous, as is the parsnip-like root.

Ancient governments sometimes gave hemlock to criminals to drink as a form of execution. Socrates was condemned to end his life by drinking hemlock. The authorities also offered it to crucified malefactors to shorten their suffering. That may have been the reason why the Roman soldiers gave the gall to Christ, but He smelled or tasted it and refused to drink it.

HENBANE (shikron, shikrona); *Hyoscyamus aureus. 24"*

The Hebrew word *Shikron* appears in Joshua 15:11 as the name of a town that served to locate part of the boundary of Judah in newly occupied Canaan. *Shicrona* is the Hebrew name of a plant of the nightshade family common throughout most of the desert areas of Palestine, especially in the vicinity of Shikron.

The plant received its English name because of the poisonous nature of several of its species, and the fact that it sometimes caused fatalities among poultry. People in some countries smoke the dried seeds and capsules as a remedy for toothache, and it has otherwise been used medicinally for centuries. Even today opthalmologists employ an alkaloid, hyoscyamine, made from the leaves and seeds of the henbane, to dilate the pupils of the eyes to better examine them.

Henbane often grows in cracks in stone walls or old ruins, but it also frequents waste places along roadsides, where it can reach up to three feet tall at times. It has hairy, tomato-like leaves, and the *aureus* species has showy yellow blossoms with purple throats and anthers.

HENNA (kopher); *Lawsonia inermis.* 10′

The KJV renders the Hebrew word *kopher* in Songs of Solomon 1:14 and 4:13 as "camphire" (margin, "cypress"): "My beloved is unto me as a cluster of camphire in the vineyards of Engedi." Recent translations more correctly give it as "cluster of henna blossoms." It is the only direct reference to henna in the Bible.

Henna is a privet-like shrub in the loosestrife family that bears large clusters of strongly scented yellow or white flowers from which one can distill a perfume. The Arabs use the bark for medicinal purposes, and the ancient Egyptians made a yellow dye from the leaves to dye the fabric in which they wrapped their mummies. It also provided, and still does provide, a hair dye and coloring for the fingers, toenails, and the palms of the hands in some countries.

Some commentators believe that the instruction given in Deuteronomy 21:11, 12 about shearing the hair and paring the nails of a woman taken in battle before she could become the wife of the captor may have had to do with the custom of henna dyeing, and Israelites were to do it to remove this evidence of paganism from her.

Henna grows naturally in the tropics of Africa and the Middle East into India, but has been widely planted elsewhere. In Palestine it grows in the lower Jordan valley and the coastal plain, but it has now vanished from the region around Engedi.

LADANUM; labdanum (lot); *Cistus incanus. 26"*

The KJV has incorrectly translated the Hebrew *lot* in Genesis 37:25 as "myrrh." The Ishmaelites to whom his brothers sold Joseph were carrying "gum [margin], balm, and myrrh" with them on their way to Egypt. When the brothers later went to Egypt on their second trip for grain during the famine, they took a gift for the ruler that included some "myrrh" (Genesis 43:11). Though not really myrrh, it was evidently a precious enough substance to present to Pharaoh. All the other items were native to Canaan, but myrrh is tropical in origin. For this and other reasons scholars and translators now believe it should have been ladanum, a resin found on a desert plant of that name, also known as a rockrose.

The sap exudes on the leaves and branches and one can gather it with a rakelike tool that has leather thongs for teeth. It also collects on the beards of goats feeding on the leaves of the shrub. Still another method of harvesting it is to boil in water the branches on which it appears. The ancients valued the gum for its aroma. They employed it as a spice and prescribed it as a medicine for catarrh and dysentery. Now its main use is as incense in some eastern churches.

Labdanum is a shrub about two feet tall with small, hairy leaves and pink, roselike blossoms. Its fruiting capsules contain minute seeds. While the shrub is a dominant plant on many of the limestone cliffs of Canaan, gathering the resin is laborious and adds to the value of the gum.

LEMON GRASS—see Ginger

LETTUCE—see Bitter Herbs

MADDER, DYER'S (puah, puvah, fuah); *Rubia tinctorium.* 16″

Scripture uses the Hebrew terms for madder only as proper names (see Genesis 46:11; Judges 10:1; and 1 Chronicles 7:1). Several species of madder, however, grow in Europe and Asia and it had wide cultivation in Bible lands in ancient times. The eastern United States has a related plant, the white bedstraw. Both plants belong to the Rubiaceae family. Madder is a perennial herb with whorls of rough, prickly, lanceolate leaves, small greenish-yellow flowers, and a red, berrylike fruit.

The plant is important chiefly for its root, from which one can extract a red dye. The use of madder roots for dye began early in history. Some of the mummies in the tombs of Egypt had fabric dyed in it. Not only does it produce a brilliant scarlet, but also turkey red, pink, yellow, purple, and brown. It had an important role in the dyeing industry before the discovery of coal-tar dyes.

Madder dye colored some of the priestly garments and the hangings of the tabernacle and Temple. The scarlet cord that the harlot Rahab hung in her window in the wall of Jericho (Joshua 2:18) and the scarlet thread that the midwife tied around the hand of one of Tamar's twins at their birth (Genesis 38:28-30) were both probably dyed with madder and had symbolic meanings. Madder, when used medicinally in some countries, may turn the bones, fingers, and toenails red.

MANDRAKE (dudaim); *Mandragora autumnalis*. 6"

Genesis 30:14, 15 records the incident in which Jacob's oldest son, Reuben, went out into the fields and found some mandrakes which he gave to his mother Leah. Rachel, Jacob's second wife, then asked Leah for some of them. The latter's answer revealed the intense rivalry between the two, for she said, "Is it a small matter that thou hast taken my husband? and wouldest thou take away my son's mandrakes also?" As payment for the plants, Rachel allowed Leah to sleep with Jacob that night, and as a result she conceived Issachar, Jacob's fifth son.

This stemless plant with a rosette of wrinkled leaves, ripening about the time of the wheat harvest in late spring, has a heavy, carrotlike root that often divides in two like the legs of a man. The split root, together with the strong smell and narcotic properties, has given rise to some strange beliefs. Folklore even had it crying when pulled up out of the ground, a belief that Shakespeare alluded to in the passage in *Romeo and Juliet*, "And shrieks like mandrakes torn out of the earth, that living mortals, hearing them, run mad." They are supposed to grow under gallows. On the other hand, many people believed that when consulted properly, the mandrake could bring good luck.

The mandrake has long been known for its poisonous and purgative qualities. People have also used it as an aphrodisiac and to encourage fertility—evidently the property that Leah and Rachel were interested in, for they both were anxious to gain Jacob's favor by bearing him sons. The Greeks called the plum-sized fruits "love apples." Recent studies have shown that they do have some value as a sexual stimulant, but that they also have just about enough sedative effect to nullify it.

The mandrake is a member of the nightshade family which contains a number of other poisonous plants as well as such important vegetables as potatoes, tomatoes, peppers, eggplants, and ground cherries. It bears small purple and white flowers on short stems that ripen into fleshy, yellow to orange berries that are presumably edible in small quantities.

MARJORAM—see Hyssop, Syrian (Thorns and Other Wild Plants)

MINT (heduosmon); *Mentha longifolia.* 24"

Mint shows up in the Bible only in the passages in Matthew 23:23 and Luke 11:42 in which Christ castigates the Pharisees for fussing about the tithing of anise, mint, and cummin.

In this case He was probably referring to *Mentha longifolia,* one of the most widely grown of the mints in the herb gardens. *Mentha sylvestris* also is abundant along watercourses in Syria and Palestine. Of the more than 3000 species of mints in the world, some of the common members that we might be familiar with are balm, horehound, catnip, spearmint, peppermint, thyme, and marjoram. These plants have square stems, opposite leaves, and usually bear small, two-lipped flowers that range from white through blue to lavender. Most mints are easy to grow in rich, damp soil. They may even be hard to eradicate once started, because plants can grow from sections of the rootstocks.

People in the biblical world used mint primarily as flavoring for meats and other foods. In addition it relieved intestinal gas and colic, and many took it for headaches and pain in general.

MUSTARD, BLACK (sinapi); *Brassica nigra.* 6'

The Old Testament remains silent about mustard, but Christ refers to it twice. In Mark 4:30-32 He compares the kingdom of God to a "grain of mustard seed which, when it is sown in the earth, is less than all the seeds that be in the earth: but when it is sown, it groweth up, and becometh greater than all herbs, and shooteth out great branches; so that the fowls of the air may lodge under the shadow of it." The Greek *sinapi* is correctly translated as mustard, and is the old genus name for the species found in the Holy Land. Another text (Matthew 17:20) refers to "faith as a grain of mustard seed."

The black mustard is likely the species Christ had in mind, for it develops into a greatly branching herb over six feet tall at times. It not only grows wild in Palestine, but people plant it as a garden herb. In early spring they eat the curly, basal leaves as greens. Then, when the main stalk shoots up, showy, four-petaled, yellow flowers cover all the branches. They mature into slender, clasping seed pods filled with small, black seeds not much bigger than pepper. One can either grind or use them whole as dressing or flavoring. An oil expressed from the seeds acts as a mild laxative. The seeds are also a main ingredient in plasters used to relieve pain.

The mustard family contains many other plants that are familiar stock in trade for the greengrocer: cabbage, cauliflower, broccoli, radishes, turnips, beets, and cress. Other members, such as wallflowers and alyssum show up among our ornamentals, and also quite a few, such as field mustard, tumbling mustard, and shepherd's purse, are just plain weeds in our fields.

MYRRH (more) (smurna, muron); *Commiphora abyssinica.* 12'

This fragrant-smelling gum found on several species of Commiphora trees receives frequent mention in the Bible. It was an ingredient of the anointing oil of the priests in the sanctuary service (Exodus 30:23-25) and a purifying and perfuming agent for women (Esther 2:12, Psalm 45:8, and Proverbs 7:17). The Song of Solomon speaks of its latter role several times. In the New Testament we find it to be one of the gifts of the Magi to the Christ Child (Matthew 2:11). The accounts of the crucifixion (Mark 15:23) and the anticipated embalming of Christ's body after His death (John 19:39, 40) refer to it.

The commiphora trees of Africa and southern Arabia are members of the Burseraceae family which includes the stubby elephant trees of southwestern America. Like them, they have small leaves and thin bark that bleeds easily. The leaves have three leaflets, the blossoms are small and pinkish, and the fruits are like small olives. Sap exudes from the twigs and branches, and one can encourage it to flow more freely by incising the bark. The tears appear oily at first, but soon harden to a whitish, brown-red resin that is fragrant and spicy.

Myrrh also appears in Genesis 37:25 and 43:11. Scholars believe that here it was not the sap of the commiphora, but ladanum instead. I have given the reasons for thinking so under that heading.

REICHARDIA—see Bitter Herbs

ROCKET, GARDEN (orath); *Eruca sativa.* 20″

Orah, Hebrew for herbs or vegetables, has also been identified with the garden rocket, a plant plentiful around Gilgal. The garden rocket is an annual in the mustard family, its lower leaves commonly eaten as greens in spring. The word occurs in 2 Kings 4:39 which narrates how one of the sons of the prophets "went out into the field to gather herbs" and came back with a batch of poisonous gourds. It may have been that the rockets were out of season at the time and he could find none of them.

The rocket is a flower similar to the ones that grow in our flower gardens. It has pale yellow, four-petaled flowers that are quite showy and attractive. The seeds of the rocket sometimes serve as a substitute for pepper.

RUE (peganon); *Ruta chalapensis.* 12″

Rue occurs only in Luke 11:42 in connection with mint and other herbs that the ancient Jews meticulously tithed. Actually, though, rue is not an herb, but a dwarf shrub native to Palestine and other Mediterranean countries. It is not related to our tall meadow rue or to the rue anemone, but belongs to the citrus family, thus is a cousin to oranges, grapefruit, and lemons. It has numerous yellow flowers with fringed petals and green calyxes that mature into seed capsules containing dark seeds. Oil glands cover the leaves, providing an oil that one can distill into an antidote for spasms and various other ailments.

SAFFLOWER—see Crocus

SAFFRON—see Crocus

SPIKENARD (nerd) (nardos); *Nardostachys jatamansi. 20″*

Spikenard, a costly ointment, appears in both the Old and the New Testaments. The ancients valued it as a perfume and used it in baths and at banquets. Imported from India, where it grew at elevations of 11,000 to 17,000 feet, this precious ointment reached the Holy Land via camel routes.

The Song of Solomon 1:12 states, "While the king sitteth at his table, my spikenard sendeth forth the smell thereof." John 12:3 says, "Then took Mary a pound of ointment of spikenard, very costly, and anointed the feet of Jesus, and wiped his feet with her hair: and the house was filled with the odour of the ointment." (Modern nostrils find the smell actually offensive, but at that time people thought otherwise.)

The other two gospel accounts (Matthew 26:6-13 and Mark 14:3-9) also emphasize the costliness of the ointment. Pliny says that the price of nard spikes reached as high as 100 dinarii per pound, the refined ointment still higher. Judas complained that they could have sold the pound of ointment for 300 pence, or dinarii, and the money given to the poor. Scholars have estimated that the real value of Mary's gift was roughly the equivalent of a workingman's annual wages at that time. Her profession was evidently more remunerative.

The spikenard is a member of the Valerianaceae family. Man cultivates other members of that family for their medicinal value. The plant has bunches of pink flowers at the top of slender stems that arise from bright green basal leaves. These, in turn, come out of clusters of hairy, dark brown spikes that emerge from heavy roots. The aromatic oil occurs in the nard spikes and roots. American spikenard, or Indian root, has no relationship to the Old World spikenard.

WORMWOOD (laanah) (apsinthos); *Artemesia herba-alba.* 24"

The Hebrew *laanah* and the Greek *apsinthos* appear in general to refer to a shrub called wormwood, although it sometimes seems to be synonymous with hemlock. One reason to doubt the translation is that wormwood is not extremely bitter. Goats eat the leaves and desert Arabs make tea of them. Its use as an antidote for intestinal worms has given it the name. The leaves are bitter enough to the taste, however, to justify the connotation of the word.

Several species of wormwood shrubs in the genus *Artemesia*, grow in the Old World, especially in the Sinai and Negev deserts. They belong to the same genus as our common western sagebrush, *Artemesia tridentata*, and are closely related to the chrysanthemums and dusty millers of our flower gardens. All are in the large Compositae family. In Europe farmers raise one of the species, *Artemesia absinthium*, commercially for the production of oil of absinthe and a green alcoholic beverage that has the flavor not only of wormwood but also of anise.

The leaves of the shrubs are usually small, much divided, grayish, and hairy. The blossoms are small, yellow, and spherical, and appear on the ends of the branches. The shrub itself is usually a heavily branched, greatly contorted mass rooted by a single stem to the ground.

Thorns and Other Wild Plants

Palestine, being a region of deserts and wilderness areas, is understandably also a land of thorns and thistles. Of the 70 species of thorny plants in the Holy Land, the Bible speaks of 20. Just which ones the 20 are is far from easy to determine. In most cases the terms are general and could refer to several different species.

When we in America think of desert plants we generally picture cacti. At times we even include them in illustrations of biblical localities. We often shoot our biblical movies in our southwestern deserts. It may come as a surprise to some to realize that the cactus family is native only to the Americas, though some kinds live in East Africa, Madagascar, and Sri Lanka. This means that they were unknown in Palestine during the biblical era. Man has introduced some, like the prickly pear and cereus, since then.

Modern native-born Jews have taken their nickname "Sabra" from the Jewish name for the prickly pear cactus, which certainly is not indigenous to Israel.

In spite of the absence of cacti from Palestine, plenty of thorny plants grow there, as we shall soon see. It is really no wonder that some have called it the "Land of Thorns."

BRAMBLE (atad, choach) (batos); *Rubus sanguineus.* 48″

In Judges 9:14, 15 the parable of the trees contrasts the strength of the lowly bramble with that of the larger trees. Isaiah 34:13 refers to the bramble as indicative of the desolation of the ancient great kingdoms. Christ, speaking of the Pharisees in Luke 6:44, says, "For every tree is known by his own fruit. For of thorns men do not gather figs, nor of a bramble bush gather they grapes."

We cannot be certain just which of the many thorny plants found in Palestine that the various passages have in mind. Some think it could be the Christ thorn, or several others, but to most of us a bramble is a blackberry bush. It could well be that, for they are common in Palestine. People also equate rose briers with brambles.

The true bramble, *Rubus sanguineus*, often grows in dense thickets along riverbanks in the Holy Land. Hooked thorns and evergreen leaves cover its canes. The pale pink flowers bloom in clusters along the canes and mature into dark, edible, compound drupelets similar to our wild blackberries.

BRIER—see Zilla, Spiny

BROOM, WHITE (rothem); *Retama raetam.* 72"

The Hebrew *rothem* appears as juniper in the KJV in the four instances that Scripture uses it. The best known is the occasion in which Elijah, fleeing from the wrath of Jezebel, sits under a juniper (broom) in the desert and asks the Lord to take his life (1 Kings 19:4). Job, in answering his friends in Job 30:4, speaks of a desperate man getting sustenance, or warmth, from the roots of a juniper. Most recent translations now render *rothem* as "broom tree," and scholars do not seem to have much disagreement on it.

The white broom is really not a tree, but a tall shrub common in the desert wadis of Palestine, Arabia, and the Sahara. It has exceptionally long roots that enable it to find water and survive several years of drought if necessary. Like other desert shrubs, it grows a few hairy leaves in winter but depends largely on its numerous greenish twigs for the process of photosynthesis. In spring white, butterfly-shaped blossoms cover its branches, then mature into small pods with seeds in them. The shrub is a member of the legume family.

BULRUSH (agmon, gomeh, suph); *Cyperus papyrus.* 9′

The term that the KJV translates as "bulrush" in connection with the story of the birth of Moses most likely refers to the papyrus. The common water plant in the Nile at the time (it is becoming rare now), it provided the raw material for mats, boxes, boats, barrels, and huts for the poor. We read of Moses' mother that "she took for him an ark of bulrushes, and daubed it with slime and with pitch, and put the child therein; and she laid it in the flags by the river's brink" (Exodus 2:3).

Craftsmen wove or tied the pithy, triangular stems of the bulrushes together in bundles, side by side, to make boats. They were not only watertight when daubed with pitch, but because of the pithy stems were quite buoyant. Thor Heyerdahl and his crew sailed from Morocco to Barbados in the West Indies in 1970 in such a boat that he named *Ra II.*

The papyrus, a member of the sedge family, grows three to 10 feet tall from horizontal rootstalks in the mud of the river and has an umbellike flower head at the top of a long stalk. To make the earliest forms of paper, the Egyptians laid its pithy cores side by side and crosswise, then pressed and dried them. Papyrus paper was quite usable, but it tended to become brown and brittle with age. Parchment made of the skins of goats and sheep later replaced it.

The lake rush, *Scirpus lacustris*, and other species of sedges could also have been included under bulrushes. The text in Isaiah 58:5 ("Is it to bow down his head as a bulrush") fits it well, for the heavy heads of seeds bend down as they ripen. One can, however, say the same thing of the papyrus. Sometimes people think of cattails as bulrushes, but we have placed them under a separate heading.

BURNET, THORNY (sir, sirim); *Sarcopoterium spinosum.* 24″

"Therefore, behold, I will hedge up thy way with thorns, and make a wall, that she shall not find her paths" (Hosea 2:6). The passage describes how desert people made hedges and corrals with thorns before the invention of barbed wire. Many native villages in Africa also used piled up thorns to protect themselves and their cattle from animal and human predators.

Scholars have identified the thorny burnet with the plural *sirim* as used in Hosea, and it fits the picture fairly well. It is a intricately branched plant, composed largely of slender, zig-zag twigs with long thorns at the joints. One can roll the dwarf shrubs together and pile them up to make a formidable barrier against an unprepared intruder. The thorny burnet is common in Palestine, especially around Jerusalem, and could have been the species used to plait the crown of thorns for Jesus at the crucifixion.

Housewives used the thorns for fuel when firewood was scarce, and they crackled under the pot like "the laughter of the fool" (Ecclesiastes 7:6).

BURNING BUSH—see Senna Bush

CALTROP—see Christ Thorn (Trees)

CAPERBUSH—see Hyssop, Syrian

CASSIA—see under Herbs and Spices

CATTAIL (suf); *Typha australis.* 6'

The Hebrew *suf* as used in Exodus 2:3; Isaiah 19:6; and Jonah 2:5 may well have referred to the cattail or just to water plants in general as they grew in marshy areas. Our familiar cattail also grows in Palestine, and it has even adjusted to tolerate brackish springs.

People weave the long, erect, straplike leaves into mats and baskets, and find numerous other uses for them as well. Americans often refer to cattails as bulrushes, but British translators tended to reserve that term for the sedges.

The outstanding feature that distinguishes this plant from sedges and other water plants is the "cattail" of brown seeds and down that projects upright from the rodlike stems. The tail has a somewhat tattered look in spring when the seeds loosen and blow away with the down attached.

CHRIST THORN—see under Trees

DARNEL, BEARDED (zun) (zizanion); *Lolium temulentum*. 24″

"The kingdom of heaven is likened unto a man which sowed good seed in his field: But while men slept, his enemy came and sowed tares among the wheat" (Matthew 13:24, 25). Scholars generally consider the tares in the parable to be darnel. An annual grass, it looks quite a bit like wheat when it first comes up. It grows almost exclusively in wheat fields. When the heads appear, they are a loose series of spikelets each bearing several grains similar to wheat. In the grains, however, lives a poisonous fungus that, can produce nausea, convulsions, and even death when ingested in sufficient quantity. This weed has long infested wheat fields in the Middle East, and some seeds have even turned up among grain stored in 4,000 year old Egyptian tombs.

Scabius is another weed found in grain. The ancient Israelites may also have included it under the term *tares*. I have described it under that head.

FLAG—see Reed

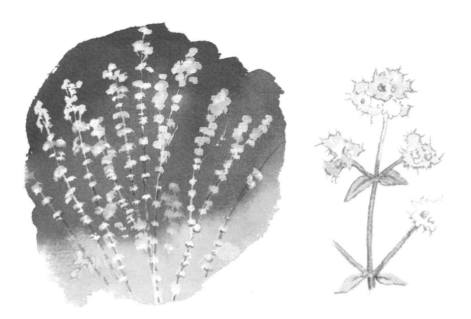

HYSSOP, SYRIAN; marjoram (ezob, zupu) (hussopos); *Origanum syriacum.* 30"

At the time of the first Passover Moses instructed the head of each Hebrew household to "take a bunch of hyssop, and dip it in the blood that is in the bason, and strike the lintel and the two side posts with the blood that is in the bason" (Exodus 12:22). This would mark the house as one the angel of death should skip during his destruction of the Egyptian firstborn during the last of the plagues preceding the Exodus.

The Israelites also used hyssop in cleansing items that had become ceremonially unclean (Leviticus 14:6, 7, 49). It was probably for this reason that David employed it as a symbol of purification when he said in Psalm 51:7, "Purge me with hyssop, and I shall be clean: wash me, and I shall be whiter than snow."

When Christ on the cross cried, "I thirst," the soldiers took a sponge "with vinegar, and put it upon hyssop, and put it to His mouth" (John 19: 28, 29). The passage gives the impression of a long stem. Some have suggested that it should have read *hussos*, which means javelin. Solomon spoke of "trees, from the cedar tree that is in Lebanon even to the hyssop that springeth out of the wall" (1 Kings 4:33). Here the term indicates a scraggly bush.

The identification of *ezob* now seems most likely to be the Syrian hyssop, or marjoram, a shrub that grows in most of the Holy Land and is, even now, used by the Samaritans to sprinkle their doorposts at Passover time. It is an erect shrub having gray-green leaves and stems covered with fine hair. Small, white flowers grow in spikes on the upper branches.

Some think that *ezob* may refer to the caperbush, *Capparis spinosa*, since it often sprouts out of walls (such as the Wailing Wall). Its showy white flowers open in the evenings. Most authorities agree, however, that the biblical hyssop is not the European hyssop, a garden herb in the mint family with square stems and a strong flavor, for it does not even grow in Palestine.

LOTUS THORN (atad); *Zizyphus lotus.* 4'

This shrub, similar to the related Christ thorn tree, thrives in the upper Jordan valley. It sheds its leaves in winter and bears small, bland fruits. Possibly it is the one used for Christ's crown of thorns, because it has not only flexible branchlets but also long thorns. Just where the name lotus came from is hard to tell, for it has no relationship to the water lily of that name or the herbs and shrubs of that name in the pea family. According to Greek legend it was the fruit of the lotus thorn that the "lotus eaters" ate, as related in the *Odyssey* of Homer and retold in Tennyson's poem "The Lotus Eaters." It had the power to make men forget their homeland and to live lives of indolence.

Another possibility for the dubious honor of Christ's crown of thorns is the caltrop, *Tribulus terrestris*, which some think is what the Bible writers specifically intended where they used the Hebrew *dardar* or the Greek *tribolis*. The thorny burnet, still another suggestion, I have covered under that name in this section.

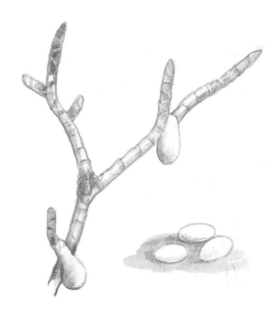

MANNA (man) (manna); *Tamarix gallica?*

Bible believers often struggle with the temptation to try to find a realistic explanation or basis for biblical miracles. It is not difficult in the case of the quails sent to the Israelites in the wilderness, for they still gather in large migratory flocks and fall exhausted after crossing the Red Sea. In the matter of the bread of heaven that God supplied to them we have more of a problem. We read in Exodus 16:14, "There lay a small round thing, as small as the hoar frost on the ground," and they called it manna, meaning "What is it?" (margin). Verse 31 says, "It was like coriander seed, white; and the taste of it was like wafers made with honey." Numbers 11:7, 8 relates that "the colour thereof [was] as the colour of bdellium. And the people went about, and gathered it, and ground it in mills, or beat it in a mortar, and baked it in pans, and made cakes of it: and the taste of it was as the taste of fresh oil." In Exodus 16:21 we also read that "when the sun waxed hot it melted." It was evidently hard during the cool of the morning.

One of the first attempts to explain this phenomenon realistically suggested that it was a lichen found in the desert that was slimy at night and hardened in the morning.

Next someone came up with the idea that manna came from a scale insect, *Coccus manniparus*, that fed on the tamarisk tree and exuded a sweet liquid that hardened and dropped to the ground at night. Desert

Arabs collect these drops and use them in place of sugar. It seemed reasonable except for the fact that few tamarisks grew in the Sinai region, and the number of Israelites was large. How long would it take to gather an omer (two quarts) of such small "tears" for every person in the camp? Furthermore, the scale insects are active only in June and July, yet the Hebrews had to eat all year.

Another plant, *Salicornica hammada*, also produced sweet drops that the Bedouin collected and made into cakes. While the plant was quite plentiful in the Arabian peninsula, it still would not provide enough to feed the great multitude that followed Moses. And it, too, was seasonal.

Manna comes also from a small, spiny plant in the legume family, *Alhagi maurorum*, that grows in southwestern Asia. The round "tears" range in size up to that of coriander seeds. They are light brown in color and would be hard to find in desert sand. Oak manna collects on the twigs of the *Quercus vallonia* and other oaks in the Mediterranean area.

We could also mention the manna ash, *Fraxinus ornus*, a commercial source of manna. It comes almost entirely from Sicily, where farmers cultivate groves of the trees. They make short incisions in the bark—whole rows, one above another—and gather the sap. It acts as a mild laxative for children. This tree, however, does not grow in the Sinai desert, and the production of manna from it did not begin until about the year A.D. 1,000.

Probably the best contenders to fit the biblical picture of manna are the tamarisk and salicornia with their scale insects, but they are hardly adequate. We will probably do best to accept it as a miracle and thus unexplainable.

On the order of Moses the priests placed an omer of manna in a golden pot kept in the ark of the covenant (Exodus 16:32-34 and Hebrews 9:4) beside the Ten Commandments, the Book of the Law, and Aaron's rod that budded. Later it was apparently removed, for when Solomon had the ark transferred to his Temple, it contained only the tables of stone (1 Kings 8:9). So the manna that was to remind all future generations of the miracle-working power of God vanished forever.

NETTLE, ROMAN (charul, seravim, gimmosh, sirpad); *Urtica pilulifera.* 48"

Several species of nettles grow in Palestine, and because of the stinging inflammation caused by contact with them, one can understand why the Bible should mention them a number of times, usually in company with thorns and thistles. The Roman nettle is said to be especially severe in the sting caused by the fine hairs on its stems and leaves.

Nettles usually sprout around abandoned buildings, barns, and in fence corners, where manure or plant growth mulch provide the abundant humus it requires for growth. Almost all the Bible texts that refer to them do so in connection with sloth, decay, ruins, etc. "I went by the field of the slothful, . . . and, lo, it was all grown over with thorns, and nettles had covered the face thereof" (Proverbs 24:30, 31). (See also Isaiah 34:13; Hosea 9:6; and Zephaniah 2:9.)

The Palestinian nettles are tall, erect, annual herbs with soft, hairy leaves and stems, much like the ones that grew in our farmyards and fence corners.

PAPYRUS—see Bulrush

REED (kaneh) (kalamos); *Phragmites australis.* 10'

The word "reed" as used in the Bible may denote a walking staff or heavy stick, but it usually refers to the long stems of water plants that are hollow or pithy in the center and round in cross-section. They seem sturdy, but they break easily. In 2 Kings 18:21 and Isaiah 36:6 Egypt is described as a bruised reed on which "if a man lean, it will go into his hand, and pierce it."

Several species of reeds in Israel could fit this characterization. The *Phragmites australis* is a common and conspicuous one. Another large one is *Arundo donax*. Usually reeds have round jointed stems. Musicians made the early flutes from them by fitting them with a membrane and holes. The Israelites also employed reeds for hedges, pens, and even hut construction.

RUSH—see Bulrush

SCABIOUS, SYRIAN (zun); *Cephalaria syriaca.* 48″

The Syrian scabious, though not cited by name in the Bible, is another noxious weed of the wheat fields that could have been included in the tares of the parable that Christ told of the sower in Matthew 13:24-30.

Scabious is a tall, branching plant of the teasel family. It does not really resemble wheat at all, except that its seeds are about the size and shape of wheat kernels. The main difference is that they are black. Since they get sown, reaped, and threshed together with the wheat, and cannot be winnowed or sifted out easily, they remain in the grain and make the flour bitter.

The only way one can get rid of them is to pick them out by hand, or pull up the plants in the wheat field. The latter endangers the roots of the wheat growing next to them. One can recognize scabious by the branching tops and the blue terminal flowers.

SENNA BUSH (seneh); *Cassia senna.* 3′

The Hebrew word used to describe the burning bush that Moses saw in the Sinai desert is *seneh*. Scholars have puzzled over the term, trying to determine what species of shrub it might indicate. Generally most have thought it to be a bramble or a rosebush, a position influenced by European and early Christian writings. Folklore has designated the bramble in the garden of the Santa Caterina Monastery at Mount Sinai as the very one that Moses saw. However, as with many so-called relics, the genuineness is greatly in doubt. Monks planted the bush, and brambles are not native to that part of the country.

Another shrub considered as a likely candidate for the honor of being the burning bush is a hawthorn, *Cretaegus sinaica*, that grows in that desert. Its berries turn red in fall, reminding one of fire, but that is rather weak evidence. Another suggested shrub is the *Acacia nilotica*, called *sunt* in Arabic, but it does not live in that desert. The *Colutea istra* grows there and bears yellow flowers in spring, but we have no linguistic or other support for its candidacy. An acacia can become infested by a crimson-flowered mistletoe, but it does not grow on Sinai.

The species of shrub given the best chance of being the real one is probably the senna bush. It is not thorny, but has many small branches, small, pinnate leaves, and showy yellow blossoms. The senna grows in the hot valleys among the mountains of the Arabian Peninsula, and linguistically could well be the one intended as the burning bush through which God spoke to Moses. Its Arabic name *sene* is similar to the Hebrew *seneh*.

TARES—see Darnel; Scabious

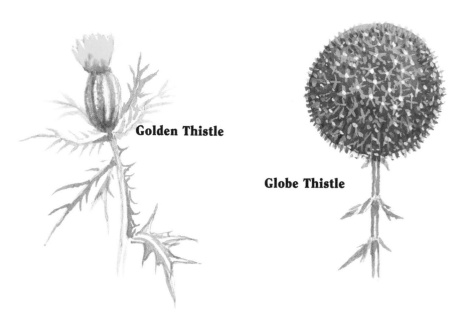

Golden Thistle

Globe Thistle

THISTLE, GLOBE (choach, hoah) (akantha, akanthinos, skolops); *Echniops viscosus.* 36″

THISTLE, GOLDEN; *Scolymus maculatus.*

THISTLE, HOLY; *Silybum marianum.*

Star Thistle

Holy Thistle

THISTLE, SPANISH; *Centaurea iberica.*

THISTLE, STAR (dardar); *Centaurea calcitrapa.*

Among the many thorny plants of Palestine we also find a number of species of thistles. Genesis 3:18 first mentions them as part of the curse that came upon the earth as the result of Adam and Eve's sin: "Thorns also and thistles shall it bring forth to thee." Scripture uses them as symbols of desolation and abandonment: "The thorn and the thistle shall come upon their altars" (Hosea 10:8). Job says "Let thistles grow instead of wheat" (Job 31:40), and Christ in His sermon on the mount, asks, "Do men gather grapes of thorns, or figs of thistles?" (Matthew 7:16).

Several species of Palestinian thistles appear in the listing above. The globe thistle is a tall, branching perennial that grows several ball-shaped flower heads of purple to lavender florets that mature into spiny seed heads. The golden thistle is a tall annual with a rigid, whitish stem and leathery leaves, both of which have rows of stout thorns. The heads are composed of showy, yellow florets. It often infests wheat fields as a weed. Another annual is the holy thistle, which starts out in spring with a rosette of large green leaves. From this, branching stems arise with white flower heads on them. The similar Syrian thistle has deep pink to lavender flower heads and more numerous, thorny leaves. The Holy Land has more than one species of star thistle. It begins life as a whorl-like cluster of leaves that lie flat on the ground. Scholars think that *dardar* refers specifically to the star thistle because the word means "whorl." They terminate in many small flower heads, each surrounded by long thorns.

ZILLA, SPINY; brier (bargonim, chedeq, sarab, shamir, sillon, sirpad); *Zilla spinosa*. 36″

The Bible speaks of briers almost always as irritating, prickly plants, often associated with thorns—they were part of the problem of living in an imperfect world. Two references (Isaiah 55:13 and Ezekiel 28:24) describe the new earth as being without briers. To the Jews, that was heaven! As we can see from the above list the KJV has translated six different Hebrew words as "brier." Naturally it is a little difficult to determine just which species the writers intended. A large number of plants growing in Bible lands could fit the context.

To most of us, briers mean thickets of wild roses or blackberries, though we usually call them brambles. They may even refer to the heath, *Erica arborea*, whose roots supply the raw material for brier pipes. Roses grow in Palestine, and we have treated them earlier under flowers, but the plants here referred to seem to be of a different type.

One that has been suggested is the spiny zilla. It is a perennial herb of the mustard family. The young plant has large basal leaves, but they become smaller as the branches grow up and out. Large pink to lavender flowers appear in the spring and develop into pointed nutlets, or pods. The plant, when mature, is a large spherical ball, densely branched and extremely prickly. With the first strong wind the main stem breaks off near the base, and the bush goes tumbling over the rough terrain, bouncing and shedding its seeds as it goes.

Trees and Vines

We do not ordinarily think of Israel today as a land of trees, except for planted orchards, but the Israel of 4,000 years ago was quite different. At times forests covered large portions of it. Some scholars estimate that perhaps up to 60 percent of the land had some kind of treelike growth. Even some of the wadis in the Negev had trees in them. The mountains of Lebanon, some 8,000 to 9,000 feet high, had extensive stands of cedars, firs, and cypresses. Oak, terebinth, laurel, olive, and carob trees ranged over much of the hill country of Judah, Samaria, and Galilee. Many locations that today are bare of trees still reflect the names of the forests and trees that once flourished there.

David as a shepherd had to guard his flock against leopards, bears, and wolves that found shelter in the surrounding forests. Lions prowled around in the shade of scattered trees, and wild boars rooted in the forests. During times when wars or captivity reduced the population, the forests increased. On the other hand, when a vigorous agrarian population prospered, the inhabitants cut the forests down and exported lumber. Hillsides were cultivated or overgrazed by multiplying flocks. The rains then washed away much of the topsoil and humus that had once supported abundant vegetation. As a result, the countryside became as barren as the hills of Gilboa.

ACACIA, COMMON (shittah, shittim); *Acacia raddiana. 20'*

"And they shall make an ark of shittim wood" (Exodus 25:10). *Shittim* is the plural of *shittah,* the Hebrew name for the acacia tree. It appears a number of times in the Old Testament, sometimes as the name of the tree or the wood, sometimes as a place name associated with the acacia trees of the region. The flat-topped, small acacia trees were common in the dry regions of Palestine, and are indeed found throughout most of the deserts of the tropical world.

They belong to the legume family and bear seeds in bean-type pods that drop to the ground where rodents and other animals and birds relish them. Gum arabic derives from certain African and Indian species. Catechu, a dye used to color khaki army uniforms, comes from another. The catclaw and mesquite of the southern American deserts are related to the acacia, and so is the attractive mimosa.

Acacias are usually shrublike in the desert, but in favorable locations they grow to be 15 to 25 feet tall. The close-grained wood of such slow growing trees is hard and has a beautiful grain. The Israelites found it suitable for much of the cabinetwork in building the tabernacle and its furniture.

Of the five species that grow in the Holy Land, the common acacia appears to be the one that would have been most suitable and available in the Arabian deserts. It has small, bipinnate leaves, globular, long-stemmed flowers and flat, twisted seed pods. The common acacia blooms in the spring and again in summer. Long, white thorns grow at the leaf axils.

ALGUM—see Saunders, Red

ALMOND (shaked, luz); *Amygdalus communis.* 20′

The fact that Jacob included almonds in his gift to the ruler of Egypt (Genesis 43:11) shows that they were known in Palestine quite early in biblical history. It seems too that Aaron's rod came from an almond tree, for it blossomed and produced the nut (Numbers 17:8). God gave Moses specific instructions to fashion the candlesticks and bowls in the sanctuary after the branches and blossoms of the almond (Exodus 25:33, 34).

Palestine has three species of almonds. The people cultivate the sweet type for its fruit and the mild almond oil that one can express from the seeds. The two wild types have bitter and inedible fruit. However, they provide hardy rootstocks on which to graft the sweet almond trees. One can express an oil from the nuts of the wild trees to use in manufacturing flavoring extracts if the prussic acid is removed.

The almond is a member of the rose family, closely related to the apricot and peach, which it resembles in appearance. It blooms early, usually in February, and the people of the land think of it as one of the first harbingers of spring. White to pink blossoms cover the trees, and if they escape damage from late frost, produce apricot-like fruits. They do not, however, mature into rosy-orange fruits. Instead the peel turns gray, and the fleshy covering dries and splits along one side, exposing the almond seed. When cracked, it releases the sweet-flavored nut.

ALMUG—see Saunders, Red

APPLE (tappuach); *Malus sylvestris. 20'*

The translation of *tappuach* as "apple" is quite likely correct. Ancient Egyptian papyri, dating from around 1200 B.C., tell of "pomegranate, apple, olive and fig trees" growing in the Nile delta. Pliny, in his *Historia Naturae,* mentions several varieties of apple as coming from Syria. Apples thrive in Lebanon today, and they grow wild in Turkey.

Deuteronomy 32:10; Psalm 17:8; and Proverbs 7:2 express the thought that God will keep His people as "the apple of his eye." The words used—*ishon*, meaning "little man," *bath*, meaning "daughter," and *babah*, for "child" have puzzled scholars. Commentators have suggested that the "apple of his eye" is the pupil or eyeball. The little man, daughter, or child may be the reflected image one sees of himself or herself in the eye of another.

Folklore almost invariably refers to the fruit with which the serpent tempted Eve in the Garden of Eden as an apple, but we have no ground for assuming that. The Scripture speaks of it only as a fruit, giving no other clue.

The writings of Josephus and others, but not the Scriptures, mention what they call the Apples of Sodom. A small tree, *Calotropis procera*, that grows in the hot deserts around Jericho may be what they had in mind. It bears twin, applelike fruits that are full of downy seeds like milkweed instead of juicy fruit pulp. The sap of the tree is poisonous. Still another plant, *Solanum sodomeum*, a nightshade and poisonous, bears yellow fruits that look like small apples. The term "Apples of Sodom" has become symbolic of something that looks desirable but proves disappointing.

ASH (oren); *Frazinus excelsior.* 75'

"He planteth an ash and the rain doth nourish it" (Isaiah 44:14) is the only mention of an ash in the Authorized Version of the Bible and its translation is in considerable doubt. Other versions have rendered *oren* as "cedar," "pine," "laurel," and "fir." The European ash, *Fraxinus excelsior*, a member of the olive family, is not even native to Palestine. The Hebrew *oren* most likely refers to the Aleppo pine, *Pinus halepensis*.

One can usually recognize ash trees by their glossy, pinnate leaves that may have five to seven leaflets; and their paddle-shaped seeds, which grow in dense clusters. A number of species are also native to America.

ASPEN—see Poplar, Euphrates

BALM (of Gilead) (seri, tzori, basam, bosem, besem); *Commiphora gileadensis. 25'*

The word *balm* occurs six times in the Authorized Version. The Ishmaelites who bought Joseph from his brothers transported "spicery and balm and myrrh" from Gilead to Egypt (Genesis 37:25). Jacob later (Genesis 43:11) instructed his sons to take "a little balm and a little honey" with the other items as a gift to the feared ruler of Egypt. Jeremiah laments, "Is there no balm in Gilead" (Jeremiah 8:22), a phrase that has become the theme of a popular hymn in more recent times. He also mentions balm in Jeremiah 46:11 and 51:8. Ezekiel 27:17 speaks of Judah trading in balm, among other items.

The balm tree is a member of the Burseraceae family which also includes the frankincense shrub and the elephant tree of the southwestern American deserts. It is a small tree or shrub that, like a number of other desert shrubs, sheds its leaves during the dry season to conserve moisture. The leaves are pinnate, composed of five leaflets. It has clusters of small, white flowers that mature into smaller-than-cherry-sized drupes, each with a fragrant yellow seed inside.

Collectors obtain the gum from cuts in the bark of the trunk and branches which bleed bright green droplets that accumulate and fall to the ground after hardening. People use the balm as holy oil, a healing agent for snakebites, and an ingredient of perfumes.

It is interesting that Scripture more than once speaks of balm as coming from the region of Gilead, an area that was then usually thought of as including the whole of Transjordan rather than only the portion north of the brook Jabbok. We have a problem here for the balm does not, and apparently did not, grow in Gilead, but rather in the hot valley to the south across the lower Jordan and Dead Sea, around Jericho and Engedi. It also ranges into southern Arabia and Somalia. Tradition has it that the queen of Sheba brought the balm tree from Ethiopia to Solomon, but it is also quite likely that it grew wild in the hot rift valley around the Dead Sea, which has a climate similar to that of Somalia.

Some have suggested that the name Gilead has been misread and should have been Gilgal, but that does not help much. Regardless of how it should be resolved, Palestine was famous for its balm, and the inhabitants jealously guarded the secret of its production.

Another tree that could well have been referred to as balm is the storax, *Liquidamber orientalis*. It is almost identical with our American sweet-gum, *Liquidamber styracifolia*, a close relative, and has the same star-shaped leaves and prickly seed balls. This tree, though rare in Palestine now, once flourished in much of Lebanon and Gilead. People collected the sap from cuts on the trunk and sold it as a potent medicine. The storax still grows in southwestern Anatolia, and the balm produced there sells as Levant Storax. It could well have been the "balm of Gilead" of Bible times.

We should mention here that the Biblical balm is in no way related to the American bee balm, or to the balsam poplar and balsam fir, all of which the American Indians and early White settlers used for medicinal purposes.

BAY TREE, GRECIAN (ezrach); *Laurus nobilis.* 45′

"I have seen the wicked in great power, and spreading himself like a green bay tree" (Psalm 37:35). In the one mention of the bay tree in the Authorized Version, its translation is dubious. The marginal reading is "a green tree that groweth in his own soil," or a native tree.

Some have thought that if the psalmist had a specific tree in mind, it could have been the Grecian laurel. The evergreen forest tree grows up to 50 feet tall in rocky soil and is quite plentiful around Mount Carmel. The Greeks thought highly of it and crowned their heroes with wreaths of laurel. Its oblong, leathery leaves resemble those of its American relatives: the red bay of the southeastern United States and the California-laurel, or Oregon-Myrtle, as it is also called. The leaves of the laurel provide flavoring in soups.

Some Bible versions read "cedar of Lebanon" instead of "bay tree," but most of the recent versions say "a spreading tree," "a luxuriant tree," or "a green tree in its native soil," which is probably fairly close to what the psalmist had in mind.

BOX—see Cypress

CAROB (haruv, haruvim) (akris); *Ceratonia siliqua.* 15'

"And the same John had his raiment of camel's hair, and a leathern girdle about his loins; and his meat was locusts and wild honey" (Matthew 3:4). The locusts that John ate were probably grasshoppers (see under Insects), but it is also quite possible that they may have been the fruit of the carob tree so prolific in Palestine. The carob looks somewhat like an apple tree, but it belongs to the legume family. It has pinnate leaves with two to three pairs of evergreen leaflets on a stem, and it bears pods about eight inches long that contain sweet seeds. The greenish flowers bloom in the fall, clustered densely on short spikes, but the fruit does not ripen until late the next summer. Male and female flowers appear on different trees, and only the female bear pods.

The seeds are supposed to be about 50 percent sugar, and one can make a syrup from them. If John the Baptist lived on a diet of only carobs and honey, it must have been rather high in sugar. Tradition calls the pods St. John's bread.

The Talmud tells of a Jewish rabbi and his son who lived for 12 years on carobs while hiding in a Galilean cave from the Romans. It is quite possible that John the Baptist ate both grasshoppers and carob beans in their respective seasons, and that he varied his diet with other food found in the wilderness.

In Luke 15:16 we read in the parable of the prodigal son that "he would fain have filled his belly with the husks that the swine did eat." They were not corn husks, for corn is of American origin and was unknown in the Old World at that time. Modern translations now use the word "pods" for "husks," and many scholars believe that pigs ate carob pods, for the ancients commonly fed them to hogs and horses.

CEDAR OF LEBANON (erez); *Cedrus libani.* 80'

The Hebrew *erez* has been correctly translated as "cedar of Lebanon" most of the time in the Old Testament, but when used to designate part of the mixture used in ritual cleansing (Leviticus 14:4 and Numbers 19:6), we can be fairly sure that it is referring to trees with similar foliage such as the juniper, cypress, or tamarisk. Cedars of Lebanon did not exist in Arabia. The masts of cedar referred to in Ezekiel 27:5 were likely pine, a stronger wood.

The cedar of Lebanon is one of the four true cedars in the world. The American western red cedar, northern white cedar, and others related to them have similar characteristics of aroma, wood, and tree features, but they do not belong to the same genera as the Old World species, even though they go by the general term of cedar.

The cedar of Lebanon is a mountain tree, flourishing best at an elevation of about 6,000 feet above sea level. Large forests of it once covered the western slopes of the Lebanon mountains, but it did not grow in Israel proper. That was why the kings David and Solomon had to negotiate with Hiram of Tyre for timber to build their palaces and Temple (2 Chronicles 2:3, 8).

The young tree is generally pyramidal in shape, but as it gets older the upper branches become dense and the top rounded. The lower branches extend out widely in separated horizontal tiers so far that the diameter of the tree at the base sometimes exceeds that of the height. The branchlets are so dense that a person can stand on the lower foliage.

The wood is coarse-grained and soft, easy to work, but more useful as structural timber than cabinet wood. It was in demand for roof timbers and planks that would last for a long time. The trees themselves lived for 2,000 to 3,000 years. The great forests have almost vanished now. Only a few groves remain to give evidence of what once was. Conservationists are attempting to restore this important asset to the Lebanon mountains.

CHESTNUT—see Plane Tree

CHRIST THORN (atad) (akanthinos); *Ziziphus spina-christi.* 30'

We read in Matthew 27:29: "And when they had platted a crown of thorns, they put it upon his head, and a reed in his right hand: and they bowed the knee before him, and mocked him, saying, Hail, King of the Jews!" Through the centuries many have speculated just which species of the many thorns that grow in the Holy Land the Romans used for this crown. Christian tradition says that the soldiers made it of the thorny twigs of the Christ thorn and that it received its name for that reason. Tradition, however, has often been wrong.

The Christ thorn is a tree that grows up to 30 feet tall and ranges over most of Israel. A few still dot the slopes of Mount Moriah near Jerusalem. The twigs are flexible and the leaves are similar to those of the laurel used to crown heroes. Yellow-green flowers bloom most of the year and mature into yellow, cherry-sized berries that are edible but not very tasty. Some feel that it might be the bramble in the parable of the trees recorded in Judges 9:8-15. The fact that the fruit of the Christ thorn is quite inferior to that of the fig seems to make it fit into that story.

CITRON (etz hadar); *Citrus medica.* 10'

This small, thorny tree, a member of the same family as the orange and grapefruit, does not appear by name in the Authorized Version, but some scholars believe that the "goodly trees" mentioned in Leviticus 23:40 should have been citron trees, one of the four species used ceremonially during the Feast of the Tabernacles.

The citron reached the Middle East from India early in history and grew in Palestine during the Biblical period. The tree has large, ovate, evergreen leaves; purple and white blossoms; and bright yellow, egg-shaped fruit six- to ten-inches long. Like the lemon, which it resembles, the peel is highly aromatic, and the pulp is strongly acid. The Corsican variety, however, is sweet. The citron has a thick rind and a small core of flesh. People sometimes candy the rind after soaking it in seawater. Supposedly it has an agreeable flavor. The Jews continue to use the fruits for ceremonial purposes.

CYPRESS, EVERGREEN (berosh, tirzah, kopher); *Cupresus sempervirens.* 40'

The Authorized Version has three references to the cypress, but two of them (Song of Solomon 1:14 and 4:13) are marginal readings. The third one (Isaiah 44:14) speaks of "the cypress and the oak." Some scholars believe that the Hebrew *berosh* is a broad term that includes several short-needled conifers like the cypress, fir, and juniper.

The evergreen cypress, is most common in the northern Sinai peninsula, but the evidence of wood fragments found in archaeological sites, indicates that it also grew in Judea. It is a columnar tree like the Lombardy poplar and some of the ornamental cypresses commonly planted now. Found in many of the Mediterranean countries, it will attain a height of 90 feet in good locations. The wood is hard, close-grained, reddish brown in color, and quite durable. Since the tree does not grow suckers from the stump it has been considered a symbol of the dead. Plato considered it sacred, maybe for that reason.

The Cicilian fir, *Abies cilicica*, grew with the cedars of Lebanon and provided construction lumber. The Israelites probably also grouped the eastern juniper, or savin, *Juniperus excelsa*, with the above. Craftsmen employed its aromatic wood for storage chests and furniture.

In the New International Version and other translations the passages referred to in the Song of Solomon render the Hebrew *kopher* as "henna" instead of "camphire" or "cypress." There is evidently a good philological basis for thinking that it is the tree from which the ancients extracted the henna dye referred to here. This is the only Biblical reference to it. For more information on it, see Henna under Herbs and Spices.

EBONY (hovenim, hobnim); *Diospyros ebenum.* 40′

Ezekiel 27:15 tells us that merchants of Dedan, near the Red Sea coast of the Arabian Peninsula, brought ivory tusks and ebony wood for the men of Tyre. The two substances, white ivory and black ebony, provided material for inlay work like some of those found in Ahab's "house of ivory."

Ebony grows in India, Ceylon, Madagascar, and Africa as well as a number of other tropical countries, but the ones named would be those most likely for ancient traders to reach in their ships. It is a small tree with evergreen leaves, trumpet-shaped flowers, and a berrylike fruit. The wood is soft and white when young, but it hardens and turns with age to a deep brown or black. A hard gum settles in the heartwood and this not only darkens it but makes it easier to carve and work. Craftsmen used the costly hardwood not only for inlays and veneers but also for carving images and relief work. More modern uses include black piano keys, knife handles, flutes, cabinets, and ornamental objects.

The American persimmon, *Diospyros virginiana*, is a species of ebony. While it does not have enough dark heartwood to make its timber valuable, it is used for shuttles and golf club heads because it is rather hard. Its luscious fruit is reason enough to grow it.

ELM, HAIRY (elah, geshem); *Ulmus canescens.* 40'

The KJV refers to the elm by name only once (Hosea 4:13): "They sacrifice upon the tops of the mountains, and burn incense upon the hills, under oaks and poplars and elms, because the shadow thereof is good." The elm may have a good shadow, but it is doubtful whether it is the one intended here.

The only elms that survive in Palestine today are the hairy elms. They still hang on in Galilee and Samaria because they grow along streams rather than on the tops of hills. One can recognize elms by their heavily veined, doubly serrated leaves, and by their fruits which are samaras with short wings curved around opposite sides of a small nutlet.

In Isaiah 44:14 ("He heweth down the cedars, and taketh the cypress and the oak") some believe that we should read "elm" instead of "cypress."

FIG (teenah, teenim, debela, pag, bikkurah) (suke, sukon, ol-unthos); *Ficus carica*. 25′

The first plant mentioned by name in the Bible is the fig (Genesis 3:7). Adam and Eve, after they had sinned, sewed fig leaves together to cover their nakedness. The fig, a member of the mulberry family, is native to the area around the Mediterranean and still grows wild in much of Palestine. On rocky hillsides it sometimes develops in a vinelike manner, but on good soil it produces a vigorous tree up to 30 feet tall. Some forest species reach even taller.

The fig was important to the Israelites in Palestine. Usually Bible writers coupled it with the vine as being representative of the prosperity that could come as a result of obedience to God. We read in 1 Kings 4:25; that Judah and Israel "dwelt safely, every man under his vine and under his fig tree." Isaiah 36:16; Amos 4:9; Joel 1:7; Micah 4:4; and Zechariah 3:10 use similar language.

Widely cultivated in Israel, figs bear two crops a year. The first crop grows on the old wood and matures in June. It is one of the earliest crops harvested each season. Later, in August and September, the big crop comes on the new growth of branches. The farmers dry and preserve much of the second crop for winter.

In spring the new figs come out on the twigs even before the leaves do, a fact that casts light on one of Christ's miracles. He saw a fig tree in full leaf in spring and expected to find mature fruit on it, but was disappointed. Being in leaf the fruit should have been there. Then He cursed the tree to illustrate to His disciples the importance of bearing fruit, not just appearing to be fruitful (Mark 11:12, 13).

FIR, CICILIAN—see Cypress

GOPHER WOOD (ase gopher, giparu).

According to Genesis 6:14, God told Noah to use an unidentified wood in building the ark. Some scholars have suggested that it may have been acacia. It is doubtful whether such a tree would have been ideal for building so huge a boat unless ancient acacias were many times taller and straighter than they are now. Others have suggested cypress, and this seems a bit more plausible, depending upon what species of cypress was available. Translators of the KJV dodged the issue by a transliteration of the Hebrew *gopher*. The word apparently derived from the Sumerian *giparu* and has nothing at all to do with the English "gopher."

Moses probably named the ark after the large seagoing rafts that the Egyptians used to transport obelisks and large quarry stones down the Nile. They constructed them with cedars, and it seems plausible that some such straight, knot-free, timber as cedar or redwood from pre-Flood forests would provide the material referred to by the curious term of gopherwood.

GRAPEVINE (gephen, kerem, anavin) (ampelos); *Vitis vinifera.*

The earliest reference to grapes in the Bible is in Genesis 9:20: "And Noah began to be an husbandman, and he planted a vineyard." The passage seems to infer that he acted on previous knowledge from pre-Flood times and that culture of grapes had an ancient origin. Archeology seems to bear this out.

In Israel the growing of grapes ranked in importance with the raising of sheep, judging by the numerous biblical allusions to it and the many times the prophets and Christ Himself used it as an illustration for some concept. There is no confusion, either, in the translation of the Hebrew terms *gephen*, *kerem*, and *anavim* as referring to the vine, vineyard, and grapes, or in the many other words employed in connection with the culture of grapes.

God says in Psalm 80:8-16 and Isaiah 5:1-7 that His people are like a vine brought from Egypt and planted in the good soil of Canaan. Because He had nurtured them with tender care, they should have brought forth good grapes but, instead, they bore wild, bitter ones. Christ told His disciples, "I am the true vine and my father is the husbandman" (John 15:1); also, "ye are the branches" (verse 5). He related the parable of the vineyard (Matthew 21:33-41). Both it and Isaiah 5:1-7 tell much of the culture of grapes in Bible times. They describe how the farmer planted the vine, cultivated the soil, sometimes terracing it, pruned the vine, and protected the grapes not only by a stone fence, but also a tower in which a watchman remained on duty as the fruit ripened. They also tell how laborers picked the fruit and extracted the wine.

The vineyard was an important sign of prosperity and well-being among the Hebrews. Several times we read texts similar to the one in Micah 4:4: "They shall sit every man under his vine and under his fig tree." The twelve spies came back from the Vale of Eshcol in Canaan with a cluster of grapes so large it took two men to carry it on a pole between them (Numbers 13:23). Jezebel had Naboth killed because he owned a vineyard that her husband wanted badly (1 Kings 21:1-16). Laws regulated the gleaning of the leftover grapes in vineyards, leaving them for the poor (Isaiah 17:6; 24:13). To symbolize a land stripped in wartime, Scripture says that not a single grape remained on the vines (Jeremiah 8:13).

Wild grapes in our woods often climb up high into large forest trees. They did so in Palestine also, but when there were no trees they trailed along on the ground. In many of the Palestinian vineyards the growers pruned their vines so that the central trunk grew up a foot or two, and then they let the branches trail on the ground because of a shortage of stakes to support them. But when the vinedressers did have wood they built trellises for the vines to climb on.

We read much in the Bible about the pruning of grapevines. The ancient husbandman evidently knew the value of cutting back the vines in order to get full clusters of grapes. Spraying with insecticides was apparently not necessary in those days though Amos tells (Amos 4:9) of the disaster that could come with a plague of palmerworms (locusts). In Song of Solomon 2:15 we read, too, of "the little foxes that spoil the vines." They were probably the red foxes, as distinguished from the big foxes, or jackals. It is possible, too, that they could be the small desert foxes, or the still smaller fennecs, but the latter two would not be so likely to roam in grape-growing localities.

After the Israelites had picked the grapes, they brought them in from the vineyard to the vinepress. The Scriptures say much about winepresses and the treading of the winepress. Fortunately the ruins of a number of old presses still survive today. Usually they consist of two pits hewn in rock. The pits are either round or rectangular, the upper one is larger and shallower than the lower, and a conduit connects them. The harvesters dumped the grapes into the upper pit and men or women trampled them with their bare feet. The juice flowed through the conduit to the lower, deeper pit, where the dregs settled to the bottom and the clear wine rose to the top. Here women with gourd dippers ladled the wine from the top through a cloth sieve into earthen jars. The jars, or amphorae, then went to the house where the people either used or stored the wine. As one can imagine, it would not keep long in the hot Palestinian climate without fermenting.

Both the Old and New Testaments contain many warnings about drinking too much wine "when it moveth itself aright" (Proverbs 23:31). The Hebrew term for fresh grape juice is *tirosh*, that for aged or fermented wine is *yayin*. In the New Testament the Greek term *oinos* applies to both fresh and fermented wine. The period of the grape harvest, September, was usually a time for much feasting and merriment among the Hebrews as well as other ancient peoples.

In Deuteronomy 32:32 we find a reference to the "vine of Sodom," most likely the wild gourd, *Citrullus colocynthis*. The sons of the prophets once gathered the fruit of this gourd and cooked it, to the dismay of some of the rest of them (2 Kings 4:39, 40). The only reason to confuse it with the grapevine is that it also has long, trailing runners as many of the grapes in the vineyards did then.

JUNIPER—see Cypress

LAUREL—see Bay Tree

LAURESTINUS; nannyberry (tidhar); *Viburnum tinus.* 10'

The KJV has translated the Hebrew word *tidhar* in one verse (Isaiah 60:13) as "pine tree": "The glory of Lebanon shall come unto thee, the fir tree, the pine tree, and the box together, to beautify the place of my sanctuary." In another passage in the same book (Isaiah 41:19) it is "shittah tree." Other translations render it "plane tree," "fir," and "cypress." None seem to have any sound linguistic basis for the choice.

According to Michael Zohary, the only way out is to accept the Aramaic translation of *tidhar* in the Targum Yonathan which renders it as "mornian," cognate with the Arabic *murran*, their name for the Laurestinus tree.

This shrub, or tree, locally known as nannyberry in parts of Europe and America, is a member of the honeysuckle family and closely related to the American possumhaw and blackhaw. While certainly not a lumber tree or even a shade tree, it is an attractive ornamental with its clusters of white flowers. Thus one could for that reason describe it as "the glory of Lebanon" and use it to beautify the sanctuary grounds.

MULBERRY, BLACK (baka); *Morus nigra.* 45'

Two texts in the Authorized Version refer to mulberry trees by name. In 2 Samuel 5:24 and 1 Chronicles 14:14 we read the same story of how during one of David's battles with the Philistines the Lord told him to wait for them in a grove of mulberry trees. Then, when he heard a "sound of a going in the tops of the mulberry trees," he should go out to battle. The KJV has rendered the Hebrew *baka* "mulberry" without much linguistic or other basis. Psalm 84:6 uses the word as a proper noun and the margin reads "mulberry trees." The root of the word, however, is really "to weep."

The idea of "weeping" suggests trees that exude sap and the balsam fir comes to mind because of the blisters full of sap that appear in the gray bark. The Cicilian fir of Palestine, a similar tree, may have been the one intended, though it is hard to imagine its rigid needles rustling in a "sound of a going." For further comment on the fir see Cypress.

This leads us to the balsam poplar, or balm of Gilead, as it is also known. Its leaves, like those of the trembling aspen, flutter in the slightest breeze, and they could well have given the impression of a "sound of going." For a fuller description see Poplar, Euphrates.

Black mulberries grow in Palestine, and some scholars believe that the tree is one intended in Isaiah 40:20 as the source of the wood from which the pagan made his idol. Also in Luke 17:6 it may be what Christ meant instead of the sycamine. It is hard to know for sure. Man has introduced white mulberries into the Holy Land in connection with silkworm culture.

MYRTLE, COMMON (hadas); *Myrtas communis.* 30'

After their exodus from Egypt God told the Israelites to celebrate the Feast of Tabernacles annually by living in temporary booths for seven days to remind them of the time their fathers lived in shelters in the wilderness. Nehemiah, when he brought back part of the captives from Babylon and rebuilt the walls of Jerusalem, reinstituted the feast. He had the people go out into the surrounding hills and collect branches of olive, pine, myrtle, and palm to make booths to live in (Nehemiah 8:15).

Isaiah 41:19 and 55:13 also mention the myrtle with other trees that the Lord would plant in the wilderness. They appear to be symbolic of peace, joy, and the bounteous life.

Zechariah 1:8-11 tells of how in vision the prophet saw a man riding a red horse in a grove of myrtle trees. The significance of the myrtles is not clear. It may have been just that it was a common tree in Palestine and served as an appropriate background for the more significant characters in the vision.

The myrtle tree is common over most of the Palestinian hills, being found in both Galilee and around Jerusalem. It is often a straggly shrub, but it has showy white flowers with long stamens and bears a bluish, aromatic berry used to make perfume. The craftsman uses the wood of the tree for turning and carving. In Greece and Rome the tree was important in art and poetry, heroes being wreathed in myrtle. In the Holy Land, too, it had positive connotations. Parents named both men and women after it. "Hadassah" for Esther is an example that readily comes to mind.

OAK, COMMON; *Quercus calliprinos.* 30'

OAK, TABOR (allon, ayil, elon, ayyalah); *Quercus ithaburensis.* 50'

The Hebrew terms for oak given above have their origins, in many instances, in the same roots as the word for God, because both have the characteristics of strength and stability in common. Unfortunately the KJV has also translated the terms *elah* and *aleah* as oak and caused some confusion. They should have been "terebinth" instead. Separating these references from the others, we still have a few legitimate mentions of the word oak in the Bible.

In Genesis 35:7, 8 we read of how Jacob stopped at Bethel to build an altar to commemorate the night many years earlier when he had the dream of angels ascending and descending from heaven. About this time Deborah, Rachel's nurse, died and was buried under an oak near there. Jacob named it Allon Bachuth, which according to the marginal reading means "the oak of weeping."

In the story of the disobedient prophet (1 Kings 13:14) the older prophet found him sitting under an oak tree. He persuaded the younger one to come back and eat with him, contrary to instructions from God, resulting in the latter's death.

Oaks are included among the trees that people sacrificed under (for example, Hosea 4:13), and Scripture tell us that the ancients made oars of oak (Ezekiel 27:6).

Many of the familiar passages in the Bible that speak of oaks are, however, not actually referring to that tree. We read of the angel appearing to Gideon under an oak or of Absalom hanging from an oak, but they were terebinth trees instead.

Three oak species grow in Palestine. The tabor oak is tall and widespreading, and it is likely the one under whose shade most of the activities mentioned above took place. Its oval, hairy leaves have barbed dentations, its acorns are variable, and its catkins bloom early in spring. The common oak is more often a shrub than a tree. The leaves are also oval and barbed, but smaller than those on the tabor oak. It blooms later. Both grow in groves. The large tabor oaks that stand by themselves are often remnants of earlier forests. While they are long-lived, few have survived beyond 500 years. A tree that a tour guide claims to be the precise one under which some biblical event took place is certain to be one that has grown up long after that event. Oaks once covered much of the coastal plains and Galilee, but not many of the big trees remain. Oaks are hardy and send long roots far into the earth for water. Their roots spread out horizontally at least as far as their branches do above the ground.

A third species, the scrub oak, is even more shrublike. It would not be likely to have been in the minds of any of the writers in the instances mentioned. We have referred to it elsewhere in the section on insects under Crimson Worm, a scale insect that infests these oaks and is used in the production of crimson dye.

OIL TREE (es shemen, etz shemen); *Eleagnus hortensis.* 20'

The oil tree is fairly common in Palestine. The Authorized Version mentions it once by name and two more times as the olive tree. Many refer to it as a wild olive. Isaiah 41:19 speaks of it as a tree planted by the Lord. In Nehemiah 8:15 it is one of the trees whose branches the Israelites could use in making tabernacles. 1 Kings 6:23, 31-33 states that Solomon's craftsmen employed the tree's wood for the doors for Solomon's Temple. It is hard to imagine using the wood of either the oil tree or the olive tree for such a purpose. According to Michael Zohary, we have considerable backing for translating *etz shemen* as "Aleppo pine."

The oil tree has some superficial resemblance to a wild olive, but it is actually in the oleaster family and is not an olive. Instead it is closely related to the Russian-olive (which also is not an olive) and to the gray-leaved buffalo berry of the central American plains. It has narrow leaves that are gray below and yellowish flowers that produce a heavy fragrance when in bloom. One can produce oil from its berries, that, though inferior to that of the olive, is still useful for lighting purposes.

OLIVE (sayith) (elaia); *Olea europaea.* 30′

After the fig and the unidentified gopher wood the olive is the third tree mentioned in the Bible. In Genesis 8:11 we read of how the dove that Noah released from the window of the ark, after the raven had gone and not returned, came back the second time with "an olive leaf pluckt off." The wild olives in particular are almost indestructible. If something cuts off a branch or the main trunk, new sprouts erupt. Ancient trees, some of them over a 1000 years old, still produce leaves and fruit even if they are entirely rotten inside and only a shell of bark on the outside remains alive.

The olive was a most valuable tree in the biblical world and symbolized prosperity and the blessing of the Lord (2 Kings 18:32). The ancient Israelites planted olive groves throughout almost all of Palestine, as we can see from the remains of ancient olive presses sometimes found hidden underneath dense stands of bush. Craftsmen used the wood of the olive for carving, but most of the trees cut down for that were usually already hollow inside and did not have much good lumber. It was the fruit that was most valuable.

Although the people ate some ripe olives, it was the oil expressed from the fruit that was the main product of the trees. Israelites used it in cooking, lighting the home, for anointing, as a base for holy ointments, dissolving spices, and as an ingredient in incense and aromatic perfumes.

The fruit of the wild olive was small and worthless, but their hardy rootstock served as a base to graft suckers on from good trees. The old-time husbandmen were well aware of the value of propagating by grafting. Paul refers to the practice in Romans 11:16-24, but deliberately makes a reverse application of it, having a wild olive grafted on to a good rootstock.

The olive tree is related to the ashes, lilacs, forsythia, and privet, and like most of them, it has opposite branching and leaves. Its small, leathery, gray, oval leaves are evergreen. Sidney Lanier had them in mind when he wrote of Christ in Gethsemane in his poem "A Ballad of Trees and the Master."

"But the olives they were not blind to Him;
The little gray leaves were kind to Him."

Clusters of small white flowers bloom in the spring and mature through the summer into bluish-black, one-seeded drupes that today we label as large, extra large, giant, and jumbo in the supermarkets. Although we pickle many of them in the green state and stuff them, in Bible times people usually allowed them to ripen before picking. When pickled, ripe olives have a bitter taste, but soaking them in lye solution removes the bitterness and makes them quite palatable.

In the Palestinian olive groves the harvesters shook the ripe olives off the branches or beat them off with sticks to collect them from the ground in baskets. They then went to the oil presses nearby for processing.

The reference in Job 29:6 ("the rock poured me out rivers of oil") may refer to the way the presses operated. One type had a lower millstone at the bottom of a shallow pit either hewn out of stone or built up of masonry. The stone had a heavy peg in the middle and a depression between it and the outer rim. The upper millstone was a heavy stone wheel that rolled around in the depression. The Israelite dumped his olives in at the top, then turned by either a camel, ox, or donkey that plodded around the press blindfolded, the wheel rolled around on top of them. The stone crushed the olives and expressed oil from both the flesh and the pits. The oil ran through a conduit to a cistern on a lower level. There the fibrous matter settled, and someone dipped the clear oil out with a gourd into earthenware pots to store for later use.

The Bible records a number of instances that deal with olive oil and that show its importance to the Israelites. Their cakes consisted of wheat or barley flour and olive oil. Numerous texts refer to its use in the sanctuary services. It appears that the Hebrews even managed to produce some during their wanderings in the Arabian wilderness. Samuel anointed Saul, and later David, with oil. Elijah, during the three-year drought, found a widow at Zarephath who had only a handful of meal and a little oil in a jar. It miraculously lasted them till the famine ended (1 Kings 17:10-16). Second Kings 4:1-7 presents the story of the widow of one of the sons of the prophets who was destitute except for a pot of oil. Elisha's miracle enabled her to fill enough pots of oil with it to redeem her sons from the threat of slavery.

The oil burned in the lamps of the Temple was not pressed under the wheel, but beaten carefully (Exodus 27:20). The instructions called for a careful sorting and cleaning of the olives, and under the beating the oil could flow out with less force than under the wheel, producing less oil but of a better quality.

The Mount of Olives at one time had large groves of olives on its slopes and oil presses at the foot of it. The Garden of Gethsemane in Aramaic means "oil press." The few ancient and gnarled olive trees now seen in the garden are the remnants of groves that once flourished there.

PALM, DATE (tamar, timmorah, tomer) (phoinix); *Phoenix dactylifera.* 75'

In Bible times the date palm was a common tree in Palestine, especially on the coastal plain, the lower Jordan, and the Dead Sea areas. Scripture refers to Jericho as the "city of palm trees" (Deuteronomy 34:3). One of the judges of Israel, Deborah, lived under a palm tree, or in a grove of palms, between Bethel and Ramah, just north of where Jerusalem now stands, and there she judged Israel, helped Sisera deliver them, and composed a song of victory.

Palms tolerate brackish water and can grow near salt marshes, such as around the Dead Sea. They are often the only trees in desert oases. After the Israelites crossed the Red Sea into the Sinai Peninsula they came to Elim, which had not only 12 wells of water, but also 70 palm trees (Exodus 15:27). That must have been to them a welcome relief from the barrenness of the desert.

Later in Canaan, when God instructed them to celebrate the Feast of the Tabernacles to remind them of how He had led them in the wilderness, palm branches were among those items they could use to build their booths (Leviticus 23:40; Nehemiah 8:15). When Jesus made His triumphal entry into Jerusalem the people waved palm leaves before Him and cast them before Him onto the road (John 12:12, 13). The great multitude that John the Revelator saw in vision standing before the throne in white robes held palm branches in their hands (Revelation 7:9).

Palms were important to the people of Palestine not only for the dates they gathered from them, but also for the wood and leaves they used for construction and baskets, for the shade and shelter they provided, and for their esthetics and symbolism. In the Bible they stand for final victory over all evil.

Few native palms remain in Palestine now, but conservationists have planted groves of them in regions where they once grew wild. Date palms are dioecious, male and female flowers being on different trees. If planted from seed, half of the young trees would be non-fruit-bearing males. For that reason, and to preserve the genetic purity of desirable varieties, man propagates palms by means of the suckers that grow from the roots around the base of the tree. One male tree provides enough pollen to manually pollinate a whole grove of female trees.

The juicy dates grow in clusters of 30 to 50 pounds. After they are picked, they are dried and packed. About 30 different species of date palms exist in the world, but only a few of them produce edible fruit. Dates were an important article of commerce in Bible times. Camel caravans and other travelers over the deserts found them a convenient food to take with them. They were a concentrated, nutritious food, and when dried, they kept well in the heat of the desert.

PINE, ALEPPO (etz shemen, tidhar, beroth); *Pinus halepensis.* 60′

PINE, STONE (tirzah); *Pinus pinea.* 90′

Translators have rendered so many different Hebrew terms as "pine" that it has left commentators greatly confused about the whole subject. Michael Zohary concludes in his *Plants of the Bible* that *tirzah*, as used in

Isaiah 44:14, should be translated as "stone pine" specifically. He also insists that we should render *etz shemen* as "pine" in 1 Kings 6:23, 31, 33; Nehemiah 8:15; and Isaiah 41:19 rather than "olive wood" or "wild olive," as it often is. Since he is an authoritative botanist at the Hebrew University in Jerusalem, is conversant with ancient and modern Hebrew as well as several other languages including Arabic, and has intimately studied biblical flora for 50 years, his judgment should carry some weight.

The Aleppo pine is not common in Israel now, but scattered remnants show that this "pride of Carmel" once covered many of the limestone hills. It bears two needles to a bundle and its oblong cones open after two years of maturing to release long-winged seeds.

The stone pine, that even in the nineteenth century flourished in extensive forests on the coastal plains and in Galilee, now survives only in small groves. It is a picturesque tree, up to 90 feet tall, with a bare trunk and an umbrella-shaped cluster of branches at the top. The common pine in Italy, it was, no doubt, the inspiration for Respighi's *I Pina di Roma*. The branches have needles four inches long that grow in pairs. Large, reddish-brown, oval cones contain wingless seeds that fall as the scales disintegrate. They are the pignolia nuts that have been prized as delicacies from ancient times.

PISTACHIO NUT (botnim, botnah); *Pistacia vera.* 30'

The KJV does not specifically mention the pistachio, but most scholars agree that the word nut in Genesis 43:11 refers to the pistachio nut, and most recent translations render it so.

The pistachio tree is a member of the Anacardiaceae family, to which the sumacs and cashews also belong. It is supposed to have originated in Syria or Persia, but it was introduced into Palestine early in Biblical history. The tree does not grow very tall, but has wide-spreading branches. Like the sumacs, it has pinnate leaves, but unlike them it has only three to five leaflets to a petiole. They are rather large, ovate, and leathery. The minute flowers grow male and female on different trees, and, in an orchard, one male tree is enough to pollinate about 20 females.

Sometimes people call pistachios "green almonds," but they are not related to almonds. The main similarity is that a thin, hard, outside shell splits along one side, like an oyster, without shedding its nut. The seed is single, solid, mild-flavored, and rich in fat. The outside husks are reddish in color, but the nut is greenish. The fruit grows in heavy clusters like that of some sumacs.

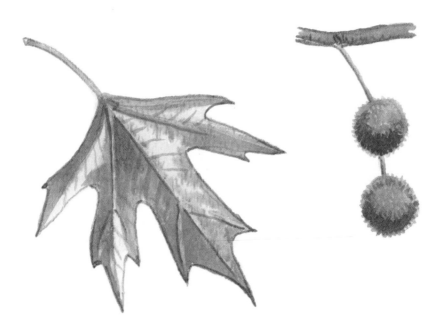

PLANE TREE, ORIENTAL (armon, ermon, tidhar); *Platanus orientalis*. 80'

The KJV translates *ermon* as "chestnut" and *tidhar* as "pine," but scholars believe that both refer to the oriental plane tree, a close relative of our American sycamore. Both trees usually prefer stream banks, and the fact that a number of wadis in Palestine bear the names of trees that no longer grow there suggests that the plane trees may have been more common in earlier times than they are now. Quite a number of them still survive along streams in northern Palestine.

Jacob carved chestnut (plane tree) stakes when he attempted to influence the color of the animals born in Laban's herds (Genesis 30:37). Ezekiel 31:8 compares the chestnut (plane tree) to the cedar of Lebanon. Isaiah 41:19 and 60:13 refer to the pine (plane tree) in a list of trees Israel would one day plant in the wilderness.

The Oriental plane tree is quite similar to our sycamore except that its leaves are more deeply indented and its seed balls grow two or more to a stem instead of singly. In this respect, it is more like California and Arizona sycamores. All of them have shedding bark that comes off in flakes, leaving creamy white to green blotches on the smooth bark. The Hebrew *armon* means "naked" and may allude to the naked appearance of the new bark.

POMEGRANATE (rimmon); *Pumica granatum*. 15′

Numbers 13:23 relates how the 12 spies brought back from the Valley of Eshcol not only the giant cluster of grapes, but also some pomegranates and figs. And in Numbers 20:5 we read the people's murmuring and complaining that the wilderness was no "place of seed, or of figs, or of vines, or of pomegranates." The Song of Solomon refers to the beauty of pomegranates. They were also important in worship. Artisans carved replicas of them on the free-standing pillars in front of Solomon's Temple, and pomegranates also hung as ornaments on the priestly robes.

The pomegranate is a small tree or bush, the only member of the Punicaceae family, though there are many subspecies. It apparently originated in Persia, but people soon propagated it throughout most of the Mediterranean countries, and Spanish settlers brought it to the New World.

Pomegranate leaves are bright green, shiny, elliptical, and about three inches long. Showy, scarlet, roselike blossoms grow at the ends of the branches. They mature into applelike fruits reddish in color with a prominent, persistent calyx. The inside of the fruit divides into several cells containing numerous angular seeds, each covered with a juicy, red pulp. The fruits, eaten raw, have a delightful acid flavor when fully ripe. People also make a refreshing drink from the seeds and rind.

POPLAR, EUPHRATES; Aspen (libneh, arabah); *Populus euphratica.* 45'

"And Jacob took him rods of green poplar, and of the hazel and the chestnut tree; and pilled white strakes in them" (Genesis 30:37). Jacob evidently found young, green poplars growing near the water where the flocks came to drink and used some branches from them together with those of two other species of trees for his experiment in genetic engineering. Most likely he employed the Euphrates poplar, or aspen, a common species along the banks of the Jordan and its tributaries and the dominant tree along the banks of the Babylonian rivers. Haran was near the source of the Euphrates. See also Poplar, White.

"By the rivers of Babylon, there we sat down, yea, we wept, when we remembered Zion. We hanged our harps on the willows in the midst thereof" (Psalm 137:1, 2). It is easy to visualize the homesick, deported Israelites placing their harps on the low branches of weeping willows on the banks of the Euphrates, but scholars tell us that the "willows" were most certainly also the Euphrates poplars, a position they base not only on linguistic evidence but habitat as well. Most recent translations now read "poplar" and not "willow." The weeping willow, we might add, is of Chinese or Japanese origin even though its scientific name is *salix babylonica*, and man did not even introduce it into Babylon early enough for it to have been there in the days of the Captivity.

In 2 Samuel 5:24 and 1 Chronicles 14:14 we find parallel narratives of David's experience in one of his battles with the Philistines. The Authorized Version states that the Lord asked David to wait for the enemy over against a grove of mulberry trees. Then, when he heard the "sound of a going in the tops of the mulberry trees," he should launch his attack against the Philistines. Scholars have suggested that the "mulberries" were actually aspens.

All poplars, including those in Palestine, have wide leaves on long stems that are flattened opposite to the plane of the leaf blade. This enables the leaf to flutter in the slightest breeze, as we can see in our quaking aspen. The "sound of a going" may well have been the flutter of leaves. The New International Version reads "balsam," but it is a bit difficult to imagine the rigid needles of the balsam fir as rustling.

The Euphrates poplar is a slender tree that reminds one of the willows in its characteristics. (All poplars belong, of course, to the willow family.) It grows along streams, and its lower leaves are linear and willow-like, while its upper ones are round and aspenlike. Remember that it was the topmost leaves that did the fluttering. It can tolerate quite a bit of brackishness in its moisture intake and often shares oases with date palms.

POPLAR, WHITE (livneh, libneh); *Populus alba.* 90′

Jacob's experiment in genetics (Genesis 30:37) involved rods of poplar, *livneh*. According to Zohary, the Hebrew word is a homonym and can refer to either the poplar or the styrax. In this case he believes it to be the white poplar because it is more inclined to grow along streams and send up suckers suitable to Jacob's uses.

Hosea 4:13 tells us how God's people wandered away from Him. "They sacrifice upon the tops of the mountains, and burn incense upon the hills, under oaks and poplars and elms, because the shadow thereof is good." In a way this would apply to the white poplars too, and some commentators have taken it to do so, but Zohary insists that here Scripture has the styrax tree in mind because it shares the company of the other trees named and grows up on the hills. The styrax is a small tree, 25 feet tall, but it has a dense, green foliage that provides a good shade. It is a member of the Styracaceae family, not too distantly related to the ebony. The small white blossoms it bears will mature into small, yellow, poisonous drupes.

The white poplar not only has white bark on its trunk and branches, but a fine white wool covers the undersides of its dark-green leaves. The tree may appear dark one minute, then a breeze lifts the leaves and the undersides show a snowy white. The blackish knots and furrowed bark of the lower portion contrast strongly with the rest of the trunk. White poplars grow in groves along hillsides and streams. They are large trees, up to 90 feet tall, with wide-spreading branches, and they too give a good shade. The leaves, in contrast to those of the aspen poplar, are three to five-lobed, like maple leaves but with more rounded tips.

SANDALWOOD—see Saunders, Red

SAUNDERS, RED (almug, algummim, almuggim); *Pterocarpus santolinus*. 20'

We read in 1 Kings 10:11, 12 how Solomon obtained from Hiram, king of Tyre, almug timbers that his navy brought from Ophir. The location of Ophir is in doubt, but it seems possible that it was either in India, southern Arabia, or Somaliland. In a parallel passage in 2 Chronicles 2:8 Solomon asks for cedar, fir, and algum trees "out of Lebanon." It is not likely that this precious wood from Ophir would grow also in Lebanon, so some commentators have suggested that the passage should probably have read, "Send me also cedar trees, fir trees from Lebanon, and algum timber."

Linguists generally agree that the words *almug* and *algum* are the same word with the accidental transposition of the *l* and the *m* and that the preferred spelling is *almug*. The red almug, now called red saunders or sandalwood, is a tropical tree that does not grow in Lebanon. Although some have suggested that it is the one intended here, no one can be certain.

The red saunders, or sanders, is a small tree with a fine grained, heavy timber that is black in the outside bastwood and ruby-red in the heartwood. It belongs to the legume family and bears yellow axillary flowers that mature into two-seeded fruit pods. Though sometimes called red sandalwood, it has no relationship to the fragrant white sandalwood, a member of the Santalaceae family.

Solomon used the almug for supporting timbers in the Temple, for inlay work on the stairs, and for the wooden parts of the harps and psaltries of the musicians. The wood has a pleasant odor that repels insects.

An alternative suggestion is that the almug is either the eastern savin (juniper) or the Grecian. Both grow in Lebanon.

SAVIN—see Cypress

SYCAMORE FIG (shikmim, shikmoth, shiqmah) (sukomorea); *Ficus sycomorus.* 50′

As Jesus passed through Jericho a short-statured man by the name of Zacchaeus, who wished to see Him, "climbed up into a sycomore tree to see him" (Luke 19:4). We find, too, that the prophet Amos described himself (Amos 7:14) as neither a prophet nor the son of a prophet, but a herdsman and a "gatherer of sycomore fruit." The Bible contains several other references to the sycamore. There seems to be little doubt that translators have correctly rendered the original terms, but our more recent nomenclature has created some confusion, especially in America.

The North American sycamore, *Platanus occidentalis*, is a plane tree. It is a giant deciduous tree growing over 100 feet tall and having a wide-spreading crown and a trunk with a diameter up to 10 feet. Three species grow in the United States and more in other parts of the world. The biblical sycamore is actually a fig tree, as the scientific name implies, and for that reason it is referred to as a sycamore fig. Sycamore has now replaced the old spelling "sycomore" in most dictionaries and encyclopedias. The sycamore fig is also a large tree with wide-spreading, heavy, horizontal branches near the base. That made it easy for Zacchaeus to climb. Its mulberry-like leaves are evergreen and its fruit grows in datelike clusters out of the heavy branches. The figs are smaller than the domestic varieties and not nearly as sweet, but the poor will eat them.

Like other figs, they must have certain wasps pollinate them in order to ripen. However, in the case of the sycamore fig, the pollinated fruit becomes a gall and thus inedible. To avoid this, man learned in ancient times to cut each fig with a special knife before it matured, then it ripened properly. This was the work of Amos, the "dresser" (as more recent translations have it) of sycamore fruit. The wood of the tree is porous and light, yet strong, and people value the tree more for its timber than for its fruit.

TAMARISK, LEAFLESS (eshel); *Tamarix aphylla*. 30'

The KJV does not refer to the tamarisk tree by name, but more recent versions do use the term with justification. In Genesis 21:33 we read of Abraham planting a tree, or a grove of trees, at Beersheba. The Hebrew word used for tree, eshel, denotes the tamarisk. In 1 Samuel 22:6 one can also substitute tamarisk for tree. Saul rested under a tamarisk in his pursuit of David.

This tree can grow in the hot, sandy, salty deserts and provides both shade and browsing for the desert dwellers and their flocks. No wonder Abraham planted a grove of them at Beersheba. One can easily propagate them by cuttings. Tamarisks are common in the desert wadis of most of the Negev. They usually grow no taller than 30 feet, but the spreading crown provides a cooling shade.

Twelve different species inhabit Palestine. The tallest is the *Tamarix articulata*. The leafless tamarisk carries on the processes of photosynthesis and respiration by means of the finely divided, grayish-green twigs which lose little moisture. Other species also have profusely divided twigs, and they bear small pink flowers in heavy clusters. The fruit is a small, round seed capsule. Americans have introduced some tamarisks into the Southwestern states as ornamentals.

TEIL—see Terebinth

TEREBINTH, ATLANTIC (elah, alah); *Pistacia atlantica.* 40′

The Authorized Version of the Bible does not cite this tree by name though it should have. In Isaiah 6:13 translators should have rendered the word *teil* as "terebinth," as more modern versions do. According to Michael Zohary, much confusion in other texts has also resulted from the translation of *elah* and *alah* as "oak" when they should have been "terebinth."

So we have Jacob (Genesis 35:4) hiding all of Laban's household idols and his wives' jewelry under a terebinth near Shechem as he traveled to Bethel to worship. We also have Joshua writing up his admonitions to the people on a great stone that he had set up under a terebinth not far from Shechem, where the Israelites had pitched the sanctuary (Joshua 24:26). Still later (Judges 9:6), we find Abimelech made king by a pillar under the terebinth near Shechem.

David killed Goliath in the Valley of Elah, which means terebinth. Saul and his sons were buried under a terebinth at Jabesh (1 Samuel 31:13), and Absalom, David's rebellious son, died after his head caught in the branches of a terebinth.

Of the four species of terebinth found in Palestine, the Atlantic and the Palestine are the species most likely to have been the ones referred to in the above instances. The Atlantic terebinth can grow into a large tree with wide-spreading branches, like some of the oaks. One will more likely find the other species in mixed woods, but the former occupies the edges of the desert and often stands alone. The terebinth trees are members of the sumac family and are closely related to the pistachios. They are deciduous and bear pinnate leaves with unevenly numbered leaflets. The fruits are small, fragrant drupes borne in clusters.

VINE—see Grapevine

WALNUT, PERSIAN (egoz); *Juglans regia.* 60′

Though not mentioned by name in the KJV, the Hebrew term *egoz*, translated "nut" in Song of Solomon 6:11, does definitely refer to the walnut. Scholars once assumed that walnuts did not grow in Palestine during Bible times, but Josephus refers to the abundance of walnut trees in the fruitful Valley of Gennesaret.

The walnut appears to have originated in southern Europe and Asia Minor and entered Palestine probably by way of Persia. There are about 40 species of walnuts in both the Old World and the New. The Persian walnut has pinnate leaves with two to five leaflets. Its flowers form catkins, and the fruits ripen in the fall. The husks dry and crack open, exposing the shell of the nut.

WILLOW, WHITE (aravah, arabah, tsaphtsaphah); *Salix alba.* 20'

The identification of the willow in the Bible is not generally in doubt except for the one reference in Psalm 137:2: "We hanged our harps up on the willows." In this case it was the Euphrates poplar, which has willow-like leaves on its new shoots and lower branches. It grows along streams and popular thought classified it as a willow.

Job 40:22 describes the behemoth (hippopotamus) lying in a stream: "The willows of the brook compass him about." The instructions in Leviticus 23:40 about the celebration of the Feast of Tabernacles included "willows of the brook" with the branches of a number of other trees that the Israelites could use in making their booths. Isaiah, speaking of the potential of an obedient Israel in some future day, says, "They shall spring up . . . as willows by the water courses" (Isaiah 44:4). In Ezekiel 17:5, 6 in the prophet's parable of the two eagles, we read that one planted a willow that turned into a vine and spread itself.

Some have identified the Hebrew *arabah* with the weeping willow, the scientific name of which is *Salix babylonica.* This species is, however, of Japanese and Chinese origin and did not grow in Palestine or Babylon during Bible times. The white willow, though, is native to that country and frequents the banks of most of the streams of northern Palestine.

BIBLIOGRAPHY

Alon, Axaria. *The Natural History of the Land of the Bible.* Garden City, N.Y.: Doubleday, 1978.

Anderson, A. W. *Plants of the Bible.* 1956.

Asimov, Isaac. *Animals of the Bible.* Garden City, N.Y.: Doubleday, 1978.

Augusta, Joseph. *Prehistoric Man.* New York: Tudor Press, 1960.

Barnett, Lincoln. *The Epic of Man.* New York: Golden Press, 1962.

Cansdale, George S. *All the Animals of Bible Lands.* Grand Rapids: Zondervan, 1947.

Clark, Kenneth. *Animals and Man.* New York: Morrow and Company, 1977.

Duplaix, Nicole. *World Guide to Mammals.* New York: Greenwich House, 1983.

Ferguson, Walter. *Living Animals of the Bible.* New York: Scribner's, 1974.

Harris, Thad M. *Bible Natural History.* 1968.

Keyes, Nelson Beecher. *Story of the Bible World.* New York: Reader's Digest, 1962.

Moldenke, Harold. *Plants of the Bible.* New York: Ronald Press, 1952.

National Geographic Society. *Everyday Life in Bible Times.* Washington, D.C.: National Geographic, 1967.

————. *National Geographic Book of Mammals.* Washington, D.C.: National Geographic, 1981.

Porter, Gene Stratton. *Birds of the Bible.* New York: Methodist Book Concern, 1916.

Schewell-Cooper, Wilfred. *Plants and Fruits of the Bible.* 1962.

Tristram, Henry B. *Natural History of the Bible.* 1888.

Wolf, Joseph. *The Dawn of Man.* 1978.

Wood, J. G. *Story of Bible Animals.* New York: Longmans, 1888.

Zohary, Michael. *Plants of the Bible.* New York: Cambridge University Press, 1982.